Business Miscellany

Business Miscellany

THE ECONOMIST IN ASSOCIATION WITH
PROFILE BOOKS LTD

Published by Profile Books Ltd
3A Exmouth House, Pine Street, London EC1R 0JH
www.profilebooks.com

Designed by Sue Lamble and BRILL
Typeset by MacGuru Ltd
info@macguru.org.uk

Printed and bound in Germany by GGP Media GmbH, Pössneck

A CIP catalogue record for this book is available
from the British Library

ISBN 1 86197 911 8

Contents

Contributors

Many people contributed to this book, as follows.

Sarah Dallas, Cities Guide editor of Economist.com: "Business etiquette".

Tim Hindle, management editor of *The Economist*: "Leading management thinkers", "Great business books" and "Business jargon".

Caroline Marshall, executive editor of *Campaign*: "Some advertising triumphs" and "Three advertising bloomers".

Bob Tricker, author of *Essential Director*: "Corporate governance: board styles" and "Games directors play".

Alexander Walsh, a freelance writer and researcher: "What companies say about themselves" and "Some business giants of the past".

Jonathan Williams and **Katie Eagleton** of the British Museum: "The oldest coins and notes" and "More money superlatives".

Simon Wright, a member of Economist.com's Global Agenda team: "Behind the corporate name", "Business blunders", "Some famous advertising slogans", "Bubbles that burst", "Bad boys … and one bad girl", "In their own words", "Behind the currency name" and "Inventors and inventions".

All other material was researched and compiled by Carol Howard, head of *The Economist* research department, Rishad Jonuschat and Christopher Wilson, with help from Andrea Burgess, Ulrika Davies, Conrad Heine and David McKelvey, all of whom work at *The Economist*.

❝ Business is really more agreeable than pleasure; it interests the whole mind … more deeply. But it does not look as though it did ❞

Walter Bagehot, journalist, author and, from 1861 to 1877, editor of *The Economist*

When firms ✹ *started*

Year	Firm	Activity	Country
578	Kongo Gumi	Construction	Japan
1288	Stora Enso	Paper	Finland
1385	Antinori	Wine and olive oil	Italy
1526	Fabbrica D'Armi Pietro Beretta	Firearms	Italy
1623	Zildjian	Cymbal makers	Turkey
1630	Kikkoman	Soy sauce	Japan
1630	Sumitomo	Conglomerate	Japan
1639	Hugel & Fils	Wine	France
1642	James Lock	Hatters	UK
1672	C. Hoare & Co	Banking	UK
1698	Berry Bros & Rudd	Wine merchants	UK
1734	Taittinger	Champagne	France
1739	William Clark	Linens	UK
1748	Villeroy & Boch	Tableware	Germany
1759	Wedgwood	China	UK
1761	Faber-Castell	Pencils	Germany
1783	Waterford	Glassware	Ireland
1786	Molson	Brewing	Canada
1802	Du Pont	Chemicals	US
1853	Levi Strauss	Clothing	US
1860	Anheuser-Busch	Beer	US
1862	Bacardi	Rum	Cuba
1867	Standard Oil	Oil	US
1886	Coca-Cola	Soft drinks	US
1892	General Electric	Electrical equipment	US
1896	Barclays	Banking	US
1901	US Steel	Steel	US
1903	Ford Motor	Automotive	US
1909	BP (originally Anglo-Persian Oil)	Oil	UK
1916	BMW	Motor engineering	Germany
1946	Sony	Consumer electronics	Japan
1955	McDonald's first restaurant	Fast food	US
1962	Wal-Mart's first store	Retailing	US
1971	Starbucks	Coffee shops	US
1975	Microsoft	Software	US
1977	Apple Computer	Computers	US

Sources: Company websites; *Centuries of Success* by William T. O'Hara; *Family Business* magazine

Oldest family firms

Year est.	Company	Business	Country
578	Kongo Gumi	Construction	Japan
718	Hoshi Ryokan	Innkeeping	Japan
1000	Château de Goulaine	Vineyard/museum/ butterfly collection	France
1000	Foneria Pontificia Marinelli	Bell foundry	Italy
1141	Barone Ricasoli	Wine and olive oil	Italy
1295	Barovier & Toso	Glassmaking	Italy
1304	Hotel Pilgrim Haus	Innkeeping	Germany
1326	Richard de Bas	Paper-making	France
1369	Torrini Firenze	Goldsmiths	Italy
1385	Antinori	Wine and olive oil	Italy
1438	Camuffo	Shipbuilding	Italy
1495	Baronnie de Coussergues	Wine	France
1500	Grazia Deruta	Ceramics	Italy
1526	Fabbrica D'Armi Pietro Beretta	Firearms	Italy
1530	William Prym	Copper, brass, haberdashery	Germany
1541	John Brooke & Sons	Woollens	England
1551	Codorniu	Wine	Spain
1552	Fonjallaz	Wine	Switzerland
1568	Von Poschinger Manufaktur	Glassmaking	Germany
1589	Wachsendustrie Fulda Adam Gies	Candles and wax figures	Germany
1590	Berenerg Bank	Banking	Germany
1591	R Durtnell & Sons	Construction	England
1595	J. P. Epping of Pippsvadr	Groceries	Germany
1596	Eduard Meier	Shoes	Germany
c1600	Toraya	Confectionery	Japan

Source: www.familybusinessmagazine.com/oldworld.html

Oldest newspapers still in circulation

Year est.	Title	Country
1645	Post och Inrikes Tidningar	Sweden
1656	Haarlems Dagblad	Netherlands
1664	La Gazzetta di Mantova	Italy
1665	The London Gazette	UK
1703	Wiener Zeitung	Austria
1705	Hildesheimer Allgemeiner Zeitung	Germany
1709	Worcester Journal	UK
1711	The Newcastle Journal	UK
1712	The Stamford Mercury	UK
1725	Hanauer Anzeiger	Germany
1737	The Belfast News-Letter	UK
1738	Feuille d'Avis de Neuchâtel	Switzerland
1740	Darmstaedter Tageblatt	Germany
1747	Press & Journal	UK
1749	Berlingske Tidende	Denmark
1750	Giessener Anzeiger	Germany
1752	Leeuwarder Courant	Netherlands
1754	The Yorkshire Post	UK
1755	La Gazzetta di Parma	Italy
1756	Northampton Daily Hampshire Gazette	US
1758	Provinciale Zeeuwse Courant	Netherlands
1758	Norrköpings Tidningar	Sweden
1761	Saarbrücker Zeitung	Germany
1761	Schaumburger Zeitung	Germany
1762	24 heures/Feuille d'Avis de Lausanne	Switzerland

Source: World Association of Newspapers

The business pre$$

Beginnings

The Economist	1843
Financial Times	1888
Wall Street Journal	1889
Forbes	1917
Barron's	1921
Harvard Business Review	1922
Time	1923
BusinessWeek	1929
Fortune	1930
Fast Company	1995

Circulation

Half-yearly results, latest available as at June 2005

	Europe	US	Asia	Total*
BusinessWeek	110,160	985,516	80,688	1,176,364
The Economist	358,053	504,590	109,178	1,009,759
Financial Times	269,885	124,579	31,906	426,369
Forbes	74,826	67,558	924,518	1,119,631
Fortune	105,945	817,218	86,292	1,145,932
Harvard Business Review	35,942	152,408	14,297	240,176
Time	555,205	4,034,061	287,043	5,241,056
Wall Street Journal	86,156	2,101,017	80,505	2,181,900

*Includes other areas.
Source: ABC

The world's **BIGGEST** firms

1993	Revenue, $bn
General Motors (US)	133.6
Ford Motor (US)	108.5
Exxon (US)	97.8
Royal Dutch/Shell (Netherlands/UK)	95.1
Toyota Motor (Japan)	85.3
Hitachi (Japan)	68.6
IBM (US)	62.7
Matsushita Electric Industrial Co (Japan)	61.4
General Electric (US)	60.8
Daimler-Benz (Germany)	59.1
Mobil (US)	56.6
Nissan (Japan)	53.8
BP (UK)	52.5
Samsung (South Korea)	51.3
Philip Morris (US)	50.6
IRI (Italy)	50.5
Siemens (Germany)	50.4
Volkswagen (Germany)	46.3
Chrysler (US)	43.6
Toshiba (Japan)	42.9

2003	No. of employees, '000
Wal-Mart (US)	1,500
China National Petroleum (China)	1,024
Sinopec (China)	855
US Postal Service (US)	827
Agricultural Bank of China (China)	511
Carrefour (France)	419
McDonald's (US)	418
Siemens (Germany)	417
Compass Group (UK)	413
Industrial & Commercial Bank of China (China)	389

2003	Revenue, $bn
Wal-Mart (US)	263.0
BP (UK)	232.6
Exxon Mobil (US)	222.9
Royal Dutch/Shell (Netherlands/UK)	201.7
General Motors (US)	195.3
Ford Motor (US)	164.5
DaimlerChrysler (Germany)	156.6
Toyota Motor (Japan)	153.1
General Electric (US)	134.2
Total (France)	118.4
Allianz (Germany)	114.9
ChevronTexaco (US)	112.9
AXA (France)	111.9
ConocoPhillips (US)	99.5
Volkswagen (Germany)	98.6
Nippon Telegraph & Telephone (Japan)	98.2
ING Group (Netherlands)	95.9
Citigroup (US)	94.7
IBM (US)	89.1
AIG (US)	81.3

	No. of employees, '000
Deutsche Post (Germany)	383
China Telecommunications (China)	371
DaimlerChrysler (US)	362
United Parcel Service (US)	355
Volkswagen (Germany)	337
Target (US)	328
Ford Motor (US)	328
Hitachi (Japan)	326
General Motors (US)	326
IBM (US)	319

Source: *Fortune*

the world's **BIGGEST** firms *continued*

end March 2005	Market value, $m
General Electric (US)	382,233.1
Exxon Mobil (US)	380,567.2
Microsoft (US)	262,974.9
Citigroup (US)	234,436.7
BP (UK)	221,365.3
Wal-Mart (US)	212,209.0
Royal Dutch/Shell (Netherlands/UK)	210,630.4
Johnson & Johnson (US)	199,711.4
Pfizer (US)	195,944.6
Bank of America (US)	178,765.4
HSBC (UK)	176,858.4
Vodafone (UK)	171,416.9
IBM (US)	165,787.1
Total (France)	148,957.1
Intel Corporation (US)	144,695.4
American International Group (US)	144,319.2
Altria (US)	135,246.1
Toyota Motor (Japan)	134,324.4
GlaxoSmithKline (UK)	134,123.5
Berkshire Hathaway (US)	134,067.2
Procter & Gamble (US)	133,697.0
Saudi Basic Industries (Saudi Arabia)	128,790.0
Novartis (Switzerland)	124,610.2
Chevron (US)	123,536.3
JP Morgan Chase (US)	123,261.1
Sanofi-Aventis (France)	119,029.6
Cisco Systems (US)	117,801.0
Nestlé (Switzerland)	110,440.9
ENI (Italy)	103,986.5
Wells Fargo (US)	101,406.9
Coca-Cola (US)	100,428.4
Royal Bank of Scotland (UK)	99,988.0
Verizon Communications (US)	98,333.7
Roche (Switzerland)	95,779.7
UBS (Switzerland)	95,069.5
Dell (US)	94,474.9
Pepsico (US)	88,993.5
Telefónica (Spain)	86,353.0

Source: *Financial Times*

2004	Revenue, $bn
Banks: commercial and savings	
Citigroup (US)	94.7
Credit Suisse (Switzerland)	59.0
HSBC (UK)	57.6
BNP Paribas (France)	57.3
Fortis (Belgium/Netherlands)	56.7
Aerospace/defence	
Boeing (US)	50.5
EADS (Netherlands)	34.1
Lockheed Martin (US)	31.8
United Technologies (US)	31.0
Northrop Grumman (US)	28.7
Pharmaceuticals	
Pfizer (US)	46.0
Johnson & Johnson (US)	41.9
GlaxoSmithKline (UK)	35.1
Novartis (Switzerland)	24.9
Roche (Switzerland)	23.2
Motor vehicles and parts	
General Motors (US)	195.3
Ford Motor (US)	164.5
DaimlerChrysler (Germany)	156.6
Toyota Motor (Japan)	153.1
Volkswagen (Germany)	98.6
Telecommunications	
Nippon Telegraph & Telephone (Japan)	98.2
Verizon Communications (US)	67.8
Deutsche Telekom (Germany)	63.2
Vodafone (US)	56.8
France Telecom (France)	52.2
Entertainment	
Time Warner (US)	43.9
Vivendi Universal (France)	28.8
Walt Disney (US)	27.1
Viacom (US)	26.6
Bertelsmann (Germany)	19.0

Source: *Fortune*

America's **BIGGEST** firms

1955	Revenue, $bn	1965	Revenue, $bn	1975	Revenue, $bn
General Motors	9.82	General Motors	17.00	Exxon	42.06
Exxon	5.66	Exxon	10.81	General Motors	31.55
US Steel	3.25	Ford Motor	9.67	Ford Motor	23.62
General Electric	2.96	General Electric	4.94	Texaco	23.26
Esmark	2.51	Mobil	4.50	Mobil	18.93
Chrysler	2.07	Chrysler	4.29	Chevron	17.19
Armour	2.06	US Steel	4.08	Gulf Oil	16.46
Gulf Oil	1.71	Texaco	3.57	General Electric	13.41
Mobil	1.70	IBM	3.24	IBM	12.68
DuPont	1.69	Gulf Oil	3.17	ITT Industries	11.15

1985	Revenue, $bn	1995	Revenue, $bn	2005	Revenue, $bn
Exxon	90.85	General Motors	154.95	Wal-Mart	288.19
General Motors	83.89	Ford Motor	128.44	Exxon Mobil	270.77
Mobil	56.05	Exxon	101.46	General Motors	193.52
Ford Motor	52.37	Wal-Mart	83.41	Ford Motor	172.23
Chevron Texaco	47.33	AT&T	75.09	General Electric	152.36
IBM	45.94	General Electric	64.69	Chevron	147.97
DuPont	35.92	IBM	64.05	ConocoPhillips	121.66
AT&T	33.19	Mobil	59.62	Citigroup	108.28
General Electric	27.95	Sears Roebuck	54.56	AIG	98.61
Amoco	26.95	Altria Group	53.78	IBM	96.29

Source: *Fortune*

BIG firms, **BIG** facts

Airbus delivered 95 aircraft in 1990, Boeing 381. In 2000 Airbus delivered 311 against Boeing's 489. In 2004 Airbus delivered 320 and Boeing 285.

Bertelsmann, a big German media and publishing group, owns Random House, the world's largest English language general trade book-publishing group, which has over 100 imprints in 16 countries, and sells more than 1.25m books a day. Also part of Bertelsman are RTL Group, Europe's No. 1 in television and radio; and Gruner + Jahr, which publishes more than 125 magazines in ten countries.

Coca-Cola products are sold in more than 200 countries, approximately 1.3 billion beverage servings per day.

Exxon Mobil produced 4.2m oil-equivalent barrels of oil and gas in 2004; BP produced 4m and Royal Dutch/Shell 3.8m.

General Motors had 12% of the US car market in 1921; overtook Ford in 1929; reached over 50% in the early 1960s; and fell to around 25% in early 2005.

McDonald's has more than 30,000 local restaurants in 119 countries, serving nearly 50m customers a day.

Microsoft's sales went over $1m in 1978; over $1 billion in 1990; over $10 billion in 1997. Revenues were $36.8 billion in the fiscal year ending June 2004.

Starbucks operates in about 9,000 locations in 36 countries; long-term target 30,000 stores worldwide with at least 15,000 outside the United States.

TTE, a joint venture between China's TCL and France's Thomson, is the world's largest TV manufacturing company, selling 18.5m colour TV sets in 2003, with a goal of 30m sets by 2009.

Wal-Mart employs 1.6m "associates" worldwide in more than 3,600 stores in the United States and 1,570 overseas. More than 138m customers visit the stores every week.

Sources: Company reports; press reports

Behind the corporate name

Behind the corporate name

Adidas The German sporting-goods firm is named after its founder Adolf (Adi) Dassler.

Adobe Named after the creek that ran past the houses of the American software firm's founders, John Warnock and Chuck Geschke.

Aldi Named after its founder, the Albrecht family, and discount: what it does.

Alfa Romeo Anonima Lombarda Fabbrica Automobili was taken over by Nicola Romeo in 1915. The first Alfa Romeo, the Torpedo 20–30hp, was made in 1920.

Amazon.com Jeff Bezos, the American online retailer's founder, originally wanted to call his firm Cadabra.com, as in abracadabra, until his lawyer advised him that it sounded too much like cadaver. So the company was renamed after the world's second-longest river, which not coincidentally also comes near the beginning of alphabetical lists.

…but it sounded too much like cadaver, **so the company was renamed**

Amstrad The British electronics company is a contraction of Alan Michael Sugar Trading, named after its founder.

Apple Steve Jobs, one of the firm's co-founders, either sought enlightenment in the orchards of a Hare Krishna commune, or tried an experimental all-fruit diet, or wanted to make a tribute to the Beatles and their business arm, Apple Corp. Apple paid the Beatles a substantial out-of-court settlement to use the name and legal disputes continue. The Apple Macintosh is named after a popular variety of American apple, the McIntosh. McIntosh Laboratory, an audio equipment firm, was also paid off for the use of its name.

Asda The British supermarket chain, now owned by Wal-Mart, is a contraction of Associated Dairies.

Aston Martin The Aston Hill races near Birmingham, where the British car company was founded, provided the inspiration for the first half of the name. This was married to the surname of the company's founder, Lionel Martin.

Atari Derives from Go, a Japanese board game. Atari is when all an opponent's stones are threatened with capture.

Audi Founded in 1909 by August Horch, who took the name from the Latin translation of Horch, meaning "hark" in English from the imperative form of *audire*, "to hear".

B&Q The British DIY chain takes its name from the initials of its founders, Richard Block and David Quayle.

BASF The German chemicals firm name is taken from *Badische Anilin und Soda Fabrik*. The company began by producing aniline and soda in the German state of Baden.

BMW Bayerische Motoren Werke was founded in Munich in 1917, originally to construct aircraft engines. The German car company's logo is inspired by a rotating propeller.

Bridgestone The Japanese tyremaker is named after its founder, Shojiro Ishibashi, whose surname means "stone bridge".

> **Ishibashi** means stone bridge in Japanese

Canon The Precision Optical Instruments Laboratory took its new identity from the name of its first camera, the Kwannon. It also represents Kannon, the Japanese name of the Buddhist bodhisattva of mercy.

Casio Derives from the name of its founder, Kashio Tadao.

Coca-Cola The name is derived from the coca leaves and kola nuts that were part of the original flavouring of the drink that was launched as a health tonic in 1885. The coca leaf, from which cocaine is produced, undoubtedly gave Coke a kick; the last traces were removed in 1929.

Daewoo Means "Great Universe" in Korean.

Danone The food firm began producing yogurt in Barcelona in 1919. It takes its name from the nickname of Daniel, the son of the founder, Isaac Carasso.

behind the corporate name *continued*

behind the corporate name

eBay Pierre Omidyar, founder of the online auction site, wanted to use the name of his internet consultancy, Echo Bay Technology Group. But Echo Bay Mines, a gold mining company, had registered the name already.

Fiat Società Anonima Fabbrica Italiana Automobili Torino was founded in 1899 in Turin.

Google The name, taken from the word googol, a vast number represented by 1 followed by 100 noughts, started as a boast about the amount of information the search engine would be able to cover.

Haribo The German confectioner derives its name from that of the founder and the home city of the company, Hans Riegel from Bonn.

Hasbro The American toy was founded by the Hassenfeld Brothers.

Hewlett-Packard Bill Hewlett and David Packard tossed a coin to decide whether the company they founded would be called Hewlett-Packard or Packard-Hewlett. Bill presumably won.

Ikea The Swedish budget furniture-maker was founded by Ingvar Kamprad whose family home was a farm called Elmtaryd, near the Swedish village of Agunnaryd.

Intel Bob Noyce and Gordon Moore had hoped to call their microchip company Moore Noyce. Improbably, a hotel chain of the same name had beaten them to it so they went for a conflation of integrated electronics.

Kodak Is called Kodak because George Eastman, the camera company's founder, thought that it sounded good.

Lego From a Danish phrase, *leg godt*, which means "play well". Although Lego also means "I construct" in Latin, the firm's name predates its introduction of construction bricks.

Lycos *Lycosidae*, the family name of wolf spiders, provided the inspiration. These spiders are excellent hunters that run after prey instead of catching it in a web.

Mattel The American toymaker's marque is a combination of the names of its founders, Harold Matson and Elliot Handler.

Mercedes Benz The German car company founded by Gottlieb Daimler and Karl Benz took its forename from the daughter of an Austrian businessman, Emil Jellinek. In 1898 he began to sell and promote their cars to wealthy clients and in 1900 invested in the company to aid the development of a new engine called the Mercedes-Benz. Mercedes was both his daughter's name and the pseudonym he used when racing the cars.

Microsoft Bill Gates wanted a name that suggested the microcomputer software that he would manufacture. Micro-soft dropped its original hyphen and went on to rule the world.

Mitsubishi The Japanese conglomerate's name refers to its three-diamond logo. It is a combination of the words *mitsu*, meaning three, and *hishi*, meaning water chestnut, a word that denotes a diamond shape in Japanese.

◆◆ The Japanese word for *water chestnut* denotes a diamond shape ◆◆

Motorola The Galvin Manufacturing Company started making car radios in the 1950s. The suffix –ola was popular in America at the time (eg, Rockola jukeboxes, Victrola sound equipment) for suggesting high-quality audio reproduction. Motorola is intended to suggest sound in motion.

Nabisco The American food firm was known as the National Biscuit Company until 1971.

Nike The American sports-equipment company is named after the Greek goddess of victory.

Nikon The original name of the camera company was Nippon Kogaku, meaning "Japanese optical".

Nissan The company was earlier known by the name Nippon Sangyo meaning "Japanese industry".

behind the corporate name *continued*

Nokia Named after a small town in Finland that was home to a successful pulp and paper company that later expanded into rubber goods before hitting on the idea that mobile phones could prove popular.

Oracle Larry Ellison, Ed Oates and Bob Miner were working for the CIA as consultants on a project codenamed Oracle. The project funding ended but the three decided to finish what they had begun and to keep the name for their software company. One of Oracle's first customers was the CIA.

Pepsi Brad's Drink, a concoction formulated by Caleb Bradham, a pharmacist, was renamed Pepsi-Cola in 1898 after the kola nuts used in the recipe and possibly to incorporate pepsin, an enzyme produced in the stomach that helps digestion.

❝ **Shell** started by selling seashells to natural-history enthusiasts ❞

Royal Dutch Shell Its origins go back to the Shell Transport and Trading Company. It was established by Samuel & Co as a business that sold sea shells to Victorian natural-history enthusiasts. Later, the company thought that there could be a market for oil, which it began to trade.

Saab Svenska Aeroplane Aktiebolaget, a Swedish plane manufacturer, launched its first car in 1949.

Samsung The South Korean electronics firm's name means "three stars" in Korean.

Seat Sociedad Española de Automoviles de Turismo was officially founded in 1950 in Barcelona.

Sony The Japanese electronic firm's name is taken both from a Latin word, *sonus*, which is the root of the word sonic, and from the expression "sonny boy", popular in post-war Japan when the firm was founded. The words were meant to show that the firm was a group of young people with energy and passion.

Starbucks Named after Starbuck, the mate of the *Pequod* in Herman Melville's whaling novel *Moby Dick*.

Subaru The Japanese car company takes its name from the Japanese for the star constellation called the *pleiades* or "Seven Sisters". The firm, with a logo incorporating seven stars, was formed by the merger of seven companies.

SunMicrosystems The firm's name originally stood for Stanford University Systems after the college where the founders designed their first workstation as students. They chose the name hoping to sell their product to Stanford. They failed to do so.

Tesco Sir Jack Cohen, founder of the British supermarket giant, began selling groceries in London's East End in 1919. Tesco first appeared on packets of tea in the 1920s. The name was based on the initials of T.E. Stockwell, a partner in the firm of tea suppliers, and the first two letters of Cohen.

Toyota Sakichi Toyoda first called his company Toyeda, but changed it after running a competition to find one that sounded better. The new name is written with eight strokes in Japanese script, an auspicious number.

Vauxhall Vauxhall Iron Works was built on the site of "Fulk's Hall", the house of a medieval knight, Fulk le Breant, on the south bank of the Thames in London in 1894. *Vokzal* is the Russian word for a train station, a corruption of the name Vauxhall. Tsar Nicholas I visited the station while touring Britain and was clearly impressed. Vauxhall cars are now part of General Motors.

> *Voksal*, the Russian for train station, comes from our *Vauxhall*

Volvo From the Latin meaning "I roll". It was originally a name for a ball bearing developed by the parent company of the Swedish carmaker founded in 1927.

Xerox Chestor Carlson invented a revolutionary dry-copying process as an improvement on current wet-copying methods. *Xeros* is the Greek word for dry.

Yahoo! The name is an acronym for "yet another hierarchical officious oracle", but the company's founders also liked the definition of a yahoo as "rude, unsophisticated, uncouth" taken from the unpleasant and savage creatures in Jonathan Swift's *Gulliver's Travels*.

The **BIGGEST** IPOs

	Value, $bn	Year	Industry	Location
Enel	16.5	1999	Utilities	Italy
AT&T Wireless	10.6	2000	Telecoms	US
Kraft Foods	8.7	2001	Food	US
United Parcel Service	5.5	1999	Transport	US
Infineon	5.2	2000	Electronics	Germany
China Unicom	4.9	2000	Telecoms	China
CIT	4.6	2002	Finance	US
Travelers Property Casualty	3.9	2002	Insurance	US
Telecom Eireann	3.8	1999	Telecoms	Ireland
Goldman Sachs	3.7	1999	Finance	US
Agere Systems	3.6	2001	Telecoms	US
China Petroleum (Sinopec)	3.5	2000	Oil/gas	China
Charter Communications	3.2	1999	Media/Cable TV	US
Prudential Financial	3.0	2001	Insurance	US
China Life Insurance	3.0	2003	Insurance	China
PetroChina	2.9	2000	Oil/gas	China
MetLife	2.9	2000	Insurance	US
Statoil	2.9	2001	Oil/gas	Norway
Genworth Financial	2.8	2004	Insurance	US
Telefonica Moviles	2.8	2000	Telecoms	Spain
Alcon	2.3	2002	Health products	Switzerland
Pepsi Bottling Group	2.3	1999	Beverages	US
Agilent Technologies	2.2	1999	Electronics	US
KPMG Consulting	2.0	2001	Business services	US
TyCom	2.0	2000	Telecoms	Bermuda

Note: IPO stands for initial public offering.

Sources: IPOhome.com; Renaissance Capital

America's **BIGGEST** bankruptcies

Since 1980	Assets, $bn	Date
WorldCom	103.9	2002
Enron	63.4	2001
Conseco	61.4	2002
Texaco	35.9	1987
Financial Corporation of America	33.9	1988
Global Crossing	30.2	2002
Pacific Gas and Electric	29.8	2001
UAL	25.2	2002
Adelphia Communications	21.5	2002
MCorp	20.2	1989
Mirant	19.4	2003
First Executive	15.2	1991
Gibraltar Financial	15.0	1990
Kmart	14.6	2002
Finova Group	14.1	2001
HomeFed	13.9	1992
Southeast Banking	13.4	1991
Reliance Group	12.6	2001
Imperial Corporation of America	12.3	1990
Federal-Mogul	10.2	2001
First City Bancorp. of Texas	9.9	1992
First Capital Holdings	9.7	1991
Baldwin-United	9.4	1983

Source: BankruptcyData.com

Selling off state assets

Amount raised from privatisation, $m

	1993	1994	1995	1996	1997	1998	1999	2000	2001
Australia	2,057	2,055	8,089	9,052	16,815	7,146	15,220	6,273	396
Austria	142	700	1,035	1,302	2,438	2,537	70	2,086	833
Belgium	956	548	2,745	1,222	1,842	2,288	10	*	*
Canada	755	490	3,998	1,768	*	11	*	*	*
Czech Rep	837	1,065	976	902	395	437	737	520	1,603
Denmark	122	229	10	366	45	4,502	19	111	*
Finland	229	1,120	363	911	835	1,999	3,716	1,827	38
France	12,160	5,479	4,136	3,096	10,105	13,596	9,478	17,438	429
Germany	73	678	191	1,421	3,125	11,357	2,754	1,750	3,343
Greece	35	73	44	558	1,395	3,960	4,880	1,384	1,305
Hungary	1,308	955	2,645	849	647	197	88	66	43
Iceland	10	2	6	*	4	128	228	1	14
Ireland	274	*	157	293	*	*	4,846	1,458	773
Italy	3,039	9,077	10,131	11,230	23,945	15,138	25,594	9,729	2,653
Japan	*	13,875	*	2,039	*	6,641	15,115	*	*
Netherlands	780	3,766	3,993	1,239	842	335	1,481	310	831
New Zealand	630	29	264	1,839	*	441	1,331	*	*
Norway	*	118	521	660	35	*	454	1,039	2,103
Poland	433	725	1,101	1,442	2,043	2,079	3,422	6,262	1,586
Portugal	422	1,123	2,362	3,001	4,909	4,299	1,620	3,256	353
Slovakia	63	415	1,004	486	11	†	†	1,313	508
South Korea	1,451	3,782	643	3,091	645	201	2,153	18	2,907
Spain	3,222	1,458	2,941	2,680	12,532	11,618	1,128	1,079	741
Sweden	252	2,313	852	785	2,390	172	2,071	8,082	*
Switzerland	*	*	*	*	*	6,442	*	*	*
Turkey	566	412	572	292	466	1,020	38	2,712	123
UK	8,114	4,632	5,648	2,426	4,500	*	*	*	*
US	*	*	*	*	3,650	3,100	*	*	*
OECD total	40,461	55,885	54,597	53,023	96,284	100,632	96,735	67,120	20,582
Global total	58,381	73,859	68,143	74,516	153,383	145,785	133,842	102,120	30,582

*Nil or insignificant
†Not available
Sources: OECD; International Financial Services, London

Largest privatisations since 1995

	Location	Value, $bn	Date announced
Enel	Italy	19.09	31/10/99
Deutsche Telekom	Germany	13.21	21/10/96
Nippon Telegraph & Telephone	Japan	13.00	16/10/99
Telecom Italia	Italy	10.83	27/10/97
Telstra	Australia	10.71	25/07/99
Telstra	Australia	10.01	17/11/97
Enel	Italy	9.63	22/10/04
Mobile telephone licence	UK	9.40	27/04/00
Yuganskneftegaz	Russia	9.33	19/12/04
Nippon Telegraph & Telephone	Japan	8.71	23/10/00

Source: Dealogic

Business blunders

America Online and Time Warner

The merger of America Online and Time Warner in 2000 was hailed as a business masterstroke for its brilliant marriage of the old technology and new. Time Warner had an extensive back catalogue of films and music, which AOL would be able to exploit through its internet distribution. America Online used its highly priced shares to create AOL Time Warner for $180 billion but the hoped for cross-media synergies failed to materialise and the collapse of the dotcom bubble wiped out much of AOL's value. The firm's shares slumped. In 2002 the company suffered the biggest ever corporate loss of some $100 billion. A year later Time Warner dropped the AOL prefix from its name.

Barclays

After criticism by a UK parliamentary select committee in 2003 for the hefty interest charged by Barclaycard credit cards, Matt Barrett, chief executive of Barclays bank, said that intelligent consumers would do well to steer well clear. He said he did not borrow on credit cards because it was simply too expensive. He also revealed that he advised his four offspring to have nothing to do with credit cards either.

❝ he advised his four offspring to have nothing to do with credit cards ❞

British Airways

At the height of "cool Britannia" in 1997, BA decided that it would chime with the trend-setting mood of the nation and announced that it would do away with the union flag that decorated the tailfins of its aircraft. At a cost of some £500,000 a time, it replaced the patriotic symbol with a series of ethnic designs that represented important destinations around the world. The change was lampooned in the press, denounced by Margaret Thatcher and proved highly unpopular with British passengers (though the airline claimed that foreign travellers liked it). Virgin Airlines, a competitor, plastered Union flags all over its aircraft to the discomfort of its embattled rival. The red, white and blue tailfin motif was later restored.

The C5

Sir Clive Sinclair, a British inventor and business man, had revolutionised the electronics business and amassed a considerable fortune with his succession of ground-breaking yet affordable devices, including watches, calculators and microcomputers. His innovative knack deserted him in the field of personal transport. The C5, launched in 1985, a battery-powered tricycle, was an unmitigated disaster.

Constructed in a vacuum-cleaner factory, it seemed to offer similar levels of roadworthiness. It looked ridiculous; factors such as safety and convenience seemed to have been barely **❝ it was about as roadworthy as a vacuum cleaner ❞**

considered and very few were sold (though it was relatively cheap). The C5 became a byword for business failure. Never one to be deterred, Sir Clive recently suggested that the C6 is on its way.

Dasani

A costly marketing push preceded Coca-Cola's launch of Dasani, its bottled water brand, in Britain in 2003. Further launches in France and Germany were stymied after press reports suggested that the "pure" water came out of a pipe in Sidcup, an unfashionable suburb on the outskirts of south-east London. Worse still, the entire British supply of some 50,000 bottles had to be taken off the shelves after a contamination scare. Despite a sophisticated purification process, the water contained high levels of bromate, a chemical linked with cancer. Despite these travails in Europe, Dasani remains one of America's most popular bottled waters.

Decca Records ... and another music misjudgment

Dick Rowe of Decca Records turned down the chance to sign the Beatles in 1962 saying "groups with guitars are on their way out", though the next year he made amends by signing the Rolling Stones. Sam Phillips, owner of a small recording company in Memphis, Tennessee, sold his exclusive contract with Elvis Presley to RCA Records in 1955, for $35,000. He missed out on royalties on the sale of more than 1 billion records.

business blunders *continued*

Hoover

The consumer electronics firm came up with a scheme to shift a surplus of vacuum cleaners and washing machines in Britain. In 1992, it offered two free return flights to Europe if customers spent just £100 on any Hoover product. Restrictive rules and the sale of extras was intended to cover the costs of the promotion. While their travel agents failed to cope with the overwhelming response, Hoover extended the promotion with flights to America. "Two return seats: Unbelievable" ran the ad's tagline. How true. Hoover was inundated by disgruntled customers, questions were asked in Parliament and a pressure group was formed. Customers started taking Hoover to court. The cases continued for six years. Some 220,000 people did eventually fly at a cost to Hoover of £48m and huge damage to its reputation.

> **two return seats: unbelievable ran the tagline. How true**

The Hunt brothers' silver spree

Bunker Hunt was one of the world's richest men through the family's Texas-based oil business but he wanted more. In the early 1970s, he and his younger brother, Herbert, made some cash when, after buying 200,000 ounces of silver, prices doubled to $3 an ounce. Over the rest of the decade they purchased 59m ounces, roughly a third of the world's supply, pushing the price to $50 an ounce and earning a paper profit of about $4 billion. But the high prices led to greater supplies of scrap silver and mining investment. In 1980 silver prices fell by 80% in a matter of days. The Hunt brothers declared bankruptcy and in 1988 were convicted of conspiring to manipulate the market.

Louisiana Territory

In 1803, the United States purchased from France the Louisiana Territory, more than 2m sq km of land extending from the Mississippi River to the Rocky Mountains. The price was 60m francs, about $15m. France acquired Louisiana after Napoleon swapped it with Spain for Tuscany (which Spain never got hold of).

Manhattan Island

In 1626 the Lenape Indians sold Manhattan Island to Peter Minuit, director-general of New Netherlands Colony, a Dutch settlement, for goods valued at 60 Dutch guilders, or $24. The goods are commonly identified as trinkets and beads, though this may be a later addition to the story. Minuit was also involved in the purchase of Staten Island in return for kettles, cloth, wampum and tools. These Indian chiefs did at least do better than thousands of others who got nothing for land later appropriated in America.

New Coke

In the early 1980s Coca-Cola executives decided that the way to fight the growing popularity of the Pepsi brand was a new formula for their soft drink. New Coke was first tested in 1985, and the company concluded that it was on to a winner. The public thought otherwise. Coke received thousands of complaints as soon as the drink was launched. These were dismissed as "relatively insignificant" at first. After three months and complaints from half a million irate customers the old

the company claimed it wasn't clever enough to come up with an idea like that

Coke, renamed "Coke Classic", was back on the shelves. Conspiracy theorists argue that it was a ruse to rekindle interest in Coke. The company claimed that it wasn't clever enough to come up with an idea like that.

Perrier

In 1990 American regulators said that bottles of Perrier were contaminated with traces of benzene, a chemical linked with cancer. The French producers of the sparkling mineral water claimed it was an isolated incident caused by the mistaken use of cleaning fluids at an American bottling plant and recalled 70m bottles in America and Canada. However, Dutch and Danish authorities also found traces of the chemical in Perrier, leading to a worldwide recall. The water firm then claimed that benzene occurred naturally in carbon dioxide and later blamed employees for not changing filters at its source in France. After the scandal Perrier's worldwide sales fell by nearly half and in 1992 Nestlé, a Swiss multinational, acquired the struggling firm.

business blunders *continued*

Persil Power

Unilever launched Persil Power in Britain as a washing powder containing a manganese "accelerator" that removed dirt at lower temperatures. Procter & Gamble, the Anglo-Dutch firm's biggest rival, conducted research that showed that far from cleaning favourite garments, the new powder rotted clothing away. A war of words ensued in the press and through advertising but eventually Unilever was forced to withdraw Persil Power.

Ratners

Gerald Ratner, speaking at the Institute of Directors in 1991, explained why he could sell products so cheaply in his chain of high-street jewellers. He said he "sold a pair of earrings for under a

the decanter was so cheap because it was *total crap*

pound, which is cheaper than a prawn sandwich from Marks & Spencer, but probably wouldn't last as long". He followed up by revealing that a decanter was so cheap because it was "total crap". Reports in the media led to the company's shares losing £500m in value. In 1994 the shops were given a new name and Ratner then left the company.

South African gold

In 1886 Sors Hariezon, a gold prospector from Witwatersrand in the Transvaal, sold his South African gold claim for $20. Over the next 100 years, mines sunk on or near his claim produced over 1,000 tonnes of gold a year, 70% of the supply of the precious metal in the West.

Topman

Topman's brand chief David Shepherd said in an interview with a trade magazine that the British clothes firm's target customers were "hooligans or whatever". He carried on "Very few of our customers have to wear suits to work … They'll be for his first interview or first court case." Retail giant Arcadia, which owned Topman, said the remarks were taken out of context.

Xerox

In 1977 the office equipment firm showed its top managers an electronic typewriter that could display written correspondence on a screen, store it with a click of a button, send it around the office and print out copies. The project had taken ten years to develop but the managers were unconvinced that it had a commercial future. Meanwhile, Apple Computer emulated much of the technology and developed the personal computer. Some 35 years earlier, IBM, Kodak and General Electric had all eschewed a new technology for rapidly reproducing copies on paper.

❝ managers were not convinced that it had a commercial future ❞

The Bible

Adam gave up the rights to the Garden of Eden for an apple. Esau sold his birthright for a mess of potage, though the extent of his father's estate is unknown.

BIG buck$$$$$

Profits and losses

Biggest annual profits, world ExxonMobil's $25.3 billion in 2004.

Biggest annual profits, UK Royal Dutch/Shell's $18.5 billion in 2004.

Biggest annual loss AOL Time Warner's $98.7 billion in 2002, after massive write-downs ($45 billion and $54 billion) on the value of America Online. Vice-chairman Ted Turner resigned. The $54.2 billion loss in the fourth quarter of 2002 was also a record.

European losses 2002 was a bad year for European companies too, with Deutsche Telekom suffering a €24.6 billion loss, Vivendi Universal €23.3 billion, France Telecom €20.7 billion, KPN €9.5 billion and Telefónica €5.6 billion.

... and in Japan Mizuho Financial Group, once the world's biggest bank by assets, made a loss of ¥2.4 trillion ($19.5 billion) in the year beginning April 2002.

Market capitalisation

The highest market capitalisation of any company was Microsoft on December 27 1999 at $615 billion. Other big caps on that day, in May 2005 and at their peaks (up to May 2005) were:

$bn	Dec 27 1999	May 2005	Peak	Peak date
Microsoft	615	278	615	27/12/99
General Electric	523	392	594	20/8/00
Cisco Systems	360	126	548	27/3/00
Intel	284	161	482	22/3/00
Exxon Mobil	281	344	406	4/3/05
Wal-Mart	309	200	284	15/3/02

Sources: Company websites; press reports; Thomson Datastream

The world's mo$t valuable brand$

	2004 value, $bn	2000 value, $bn	2000–04 % change	Country of ownership
Coca-Cola	67.4	72.5	-7.0	US
Microsoft	61.4	70.2	-12.5	US
IBM	53.8	53.2	1.1	US
GE	44.1	38.1	15.7	US
Intel	33.5	39.1	-14.3	US
Disney	27.1	33.6	-19.3	US
McDonald's	25.0	27.9	-10.4	US
Nokia	24.0	38.5	-37.7	Finland
Toyota	22.7	18.8	20.7	Japan
Marlboro	22.1	22.1	0.0	US
Mercedes	21.3	21.1	0.9	Germany
Hewlett-Packard	21.0	20.6	1.9	US
Citibank	20.0	18.8	6.4	US
American Express	17.7	16.1	9.9	US
Gillette	16.7	17.4	-4.0	US
Cisco Systems	15.9	20.1	-20.9	US
Honda	14.9	15.3	-2.6	Japan
Ford	14.5	36.4	-60.2	US
Sony	12.8	16.4	-22.0	Japan
AT&T	na	25.6	na	US

Note: Brand value refers to the economic worth of the brand name.
Source: Interbrand

The world's most admired companies

2004	Country	Industry	Score out of 10
Procter & Gamble	US	Household & personal products	8.75
UPS	US	Delivery	8.61
Citigroup	US	Megabanks	8.21
Walgreen	US	Food & drug stores	8.16
BP	UK	Petroleum refining	8.11
Johnson & Johnson	US	Pharmaceuticals	8.10
Anheuser-Busch	US	Beverages	8.09
Berkshire Hathaway	US	Insurance	7.93
Nestlé	Switzerland	Consumer food products	7.93
Illinois Tool Works	US	Industrial & farm equipment	7.92
General Electric	US	Electronics	7.83
Cardinal Health	US	Wholesalers: health care	7.81
Texas Instruments	US	Semiconductors	7.75
Alcan	US	Metals	7.71
IBM	US	Computers	7.69
Occidental Petroleum	US	Mining, crude-oil production	7.68
Lear	US	Motor vehicle parts	7.67
Lowe's	US	Specialty retailers	7.58
Northwestern Mutual	US	Insurance	7.44
Wal-Mart	US	General merchandisers	7.41
Cisco Systems	US	Network communications	7.39
Toyota Motor	Japan	Motor vehicles	7.32
United Technologies	US	Aerospace & defence	7.19
PPG Industries	US	Chemicals	7.05
Walt Disney	US	Entertainment	6.99
Fluor	US	Engineering, construction	6.95
SBC Communications	US	Telecoms	6.90
International Paper	US	Forest & paper products	6.85
Continental Airlines	US	Airlines	6.75
TXU	US	Energy	6.54

Source: *Fortune*

Britain's most admired companies ✓

2004	Industry	Score out of 90
Cadbury Schweppes	Food and drink	69.92
Unilever	Consumer products	69.37
BP	Oil	68.56
Tesco	Supermarkets	68.10
Man Group	Hedge-fund manager	67.90
Serco Group	Outsourcing services	67.37
IMI	Engineering	66.60
HSBC	Banking	66.34
Vodafone	Telecommunications	66.30
Wolseley	Heating/plumbing equipment	65.50
Greene King	Brewing	64.71
Royal Bank of Scotland	Banking	64.67
GlaxoSmithKline	Pharmaceuticals	64.33
Weir Group	Engineering	64.00
Reckitt Benckiser	Household appliances	63.80
Rotork	Valves and gearboxes	63.67
AstraZeneca	Pharmaceuticals	63.60
Rolls-Royce	Engineering	63.26
Kidde	Fire-prevention equipment	63.20
Compass	Catering	63.17
JD Wetherspoon	Catering	63.17
BSkyB	Media	63.13
Next	Retailing	63.10
Halma	Life-protection equipment	63.00
Capita Group	Support services	62.67
Tomkins	Engineering	62.50
Carnival	Shipping	62.44
Carphone Warehouse	Retailing	62.14
Berkeley Group	Building	62.13
Marshalls	Retailing	62.04

Note: The 10 largest public companies within 22 sectors rank their 9 sector rivals on a scale of 0-10 for 9 performance criteria including quality of management, marketing, and products and services; financials; innovation; attracting, developing and retaining talent; use of corporate assets; community and environmental responsibility; and value as a long-term investment.

Source: *Management Today*

What companies say about themselves

Anheuser Busch Our vision: Through all of our products, services and relationships, we will add to the enjoyment of life.

BMW Mission: To be the most successful premium manufacturer in the industry.

Carlsberg Mission: Carlsberg is a dynamic, international provider of beer and beverage brands, bringing people together and adding to the enjoyment of life.

Coca-Cola The Coca-Cola Company exists to benefit and refresh everyone it touches.

Ericsson Our vision: To be the prime driver in an all-communicating world.

Ford Our Vision: to become the world's leading company for automotive products and services. Our Mission: we are a global, diverse family with a proud heritage, passionately committed to providing outstanding products and services. Our Values: we do the right thing for our people, our environment and our society, but above all for our customers.

> **we do the right thing for our people, our environment and our society**

Gillette The Gillette Company's vision is to build total brand value by innovating to deliver consumer value and customer leadership faster, better and more completely than our competition.

Google Google's mission is to organise the world's information and make it universally accessible and useful. Our philosophy:

1. Never settle for the best
2. It's best to do one thing really, really well
3. Fast is better than slow
4. Democracy on the web works
5. You don't need to be at your desk to need an answer
6. You can make money without doing evil
7. There is always more information out there
8. The need for information crosses all borders
9. You can be serious without a suit
10. Great just isn't good enough.

Heinz Our vision, quite simply, is to be "the world's premier food company, offering nutritious, superior tasting foods to people everywhere."

Johnson & Johnson We believe our first responsibility is to the doctors, nurses and patients, to mothers and fathers and all others who use our products and services.

Kellogg's We build brands and make the world a little happier by bringing our best to you.

Levi Strauss & Co Our values are fundamental to our success. They are the foundation of our company, define who we are and set us apart from the competition. They underlie our vision of the future, our business strategies and our decisions, actions and behaviours. We live by them. They endure... Four core values are at the heart of Levi Strauss & Co: Empathy, Originality, Integrity and Courage ...

❝ people love our clothes and trust our company ❞

Generations of people have worn our products as a symbol of freedom and self-expression in the face of adversity, challenge and social change. They forged a new territory called the American West. They fought in wars for peace. They instigated counterculture revolutions. They tore down the Berlin Wall. Reverent, irreverent – they all took a stand ... People love our clothes and trust our company. We will market the most appealing and widely worn casual clothing in the world. We will clothe the world.

Microsoft At Microsoft, we work to help people and businesses throughout the world realise their full potential. This is our mission. Everything we do reflects this mission and the values that make it possible.

Nokia Connecting people has always been, and continues to be, our reason for business.

Pfizer Our mission: We will become the world's most valued company to patients, customers, colleagues, investors, business partners, and the communities where we work and live.

Philip Morris International Our goal is to be the most responsible, effective and respected developer, manufacturer and marketer of consumer products, especially products intended for

what companies say *continued*

adults. Our core business is manufacturing and marketing the best quality tobacco products to adults who use them.

Royal Mail Through our trusted brands, we reach everbody every working day in mail, parcels and express services and Post Office branches. Today, we are reinventing our business to meet the changing needs of our customers and the demands of competition. Our goal is to be the world's leading postal service.

Tesco Our core purpose is "to create value for customers to earn their lifetime loyalty". We deliver this through our values.

No one tries harder for customers
Understand customers better than anyone
Be energetic, be innovative and be first for customers
Use our strengths to deliver unbeatable values to our customers
Look after our people so they can look after our customers

❝ create value for customers to earn their lifetime loyalty ❞

Treat people how we like to be treated
All retailers, there's one team ...
The Tesco Team
Trust and respect each other
Strive to do our very best
Give support to each other and praise more than criticise
Ask more than tell and share knowledge so that it can be used
Enjoy work, celebrate success and learn from experience

Unilever Mission: To add vitality to life. We meet the everyday needs for nutrition, hygiene, and personal care with brands that help people feel good, look good, and get more out of life.

Virgin We believe in making a difference. In our customers' eyes, Virgin stands for value for money, quality, innovation, fun and a sense of competitive challenge.

Source: Company websites

Corporate governance: board styles

The leadership of the chairman of the board inevitably affects the way that the board goes about its business. Board styles vary enormously. Here are some typical ones.

■ **The rubber-stamp board** shows little concern for either the tasks of the board or the interpersonal relationships among the directors. Examples of such boards can be found in the "letterbox" companies registered in many offshore tax havens. The meetings of the board are a formality. Indeed, they are often minuted without them actually taking place. The boards of some private closely held companies also treat their board meetings as a formality; perhaps because one individual is dominant and takes the decisions, or because the key players see each other frequently and decisions are taken in the management context.

> **❝ meetings… are often minuted without actually taking place ❞**

■ **The country-club board**, in contrast, is very concerned with interpersonal relations at board level and the issues before the board may take second place. The boards of some old-established companies, which have been successful in the past, fit this model. There is likely to be a great deal of ritual about board meetings. The boardroom will be beautifully furnished, complete with sepia pictures of previous chairmen. Legends and myths surround board affairs.

■ **The representative board** places more emphasis on the tasks of the board than it does on board relations. Frequently, this type of board has directors representing different shareholders or stakeholders. The board is more like a parliament of diverse interests. Issues can easily become politicised. Board discussions can be adversarial.

■ **The professional board** adopts a style that shows a proper concern for both the board's tasks and its interpersonal relationships. A board with a successful professional style will have sound leadership from the chair. There will be tough-minded discussion among the members combined with a mutual understanding and respect for each other.

Source: *Essential Director*, R.I. (Bob) Tricker, The Economist/Profile Books

Games directors play

Although routinely presented as a serious, analytical and rational process, boardroom behaviour is often intensely political, involving personal rivalries and power plays. The games directors play include the following.

- **Alliance building** is played outside the boardroom for ensuring mutual support within. It is closely allied to log rolling.

- **Coalition building** involves canvassing support for an issue informally outside the boardroom so that there is a sufficient consensus when the matter is discussed formally.

- **Cronyism** is supporting a director's interests even though they may not be in the best interest of the company or its shareholders. For example, a director declares a personal interest in a contract in a tender being discussed by the board; he might even leave the room for the discussion. However, board members support his bid because of their relationship, even though it is not the most worthy. This is sometimes alleged to be the basis of corporate governance in Asia.

> **Cronyism... is sometimes alleged to be the basis of corporate governance in Asia**

- **Deal making** is a classic game usually involving compromise, in which two or more directors reach a behind-the-scenes agreement to achieve a specific outcome in a board decision.

- **Divide and rule** is a dirty game, in which the player sees the chance to set one director against another, or groups of directors against each other. An issue in the financial accounts might be used, for example, to set the executive directors, the non-executive directors and the auditors against each other in order to achieve an entirely different personal aim.

- **Empire building** is the misuse of privileged access to information, people or other resources to acquire power over organisational territory. The process often involves intrigue, battles and conquests.

- **Half truths** occur if a director, although not deliberately lying, tells only one side of the issue in board deliberations.

■ **Hidden agendas** involve directors' pursuit of secret goals to benefit their own empire or further their own career against the interest of the organisation as a whole.

■ **Log rolling** occurs when director A agrees, off the record, to support director B's interests, for mutual support when it comes to matters of interest to A.

■ **Propaganda** is the dissemination of information to support a cause and is seen more in relationships with shareholders, stockmarkets and financial institutions than in board-level deliberations. The regulatory authorities are likely to act if propaganda becomes excessive or deliberately false.

■ **Rival camps** is a game played when there are opposing factions on a board, in which hostilities, spies and double agents can be involved.

■ **Scaremongering** emphasises the downside risks in a board decision, casting doubts about a situation, so that a proposal will be turned down.

■ **Snowing** involves executive directors deluging an outside director seeking further information with masses of data confusing the situation and papering over any cracks.

■ **Spinning** is an art form developed at governmental level, which presents a distorted view of a person or a situation, favourable to the interests of the spinner. In corporate governance, spinning can be carried out at the level of the board, the shareholders or the media.

> **Spinning... is an art form developed at governmental level**

■ **Sponsorship** is support by a powerful director for another, usually for their joint benefit.

■ **Suboptimisation** occurs when a director supports a part of the organisation to the detriment of the company as a whole. Some executive directors suffer from tunnel vision because they are too closely involved with a functional department or a subsidiary company, and from short-sighted myopia because they will be personally affected by the outcome.

■ **Window dressing** produces a fine external show of sound corporate governance principles while covering up failures. Window dressing can also involve showing financial results in the best possible light while hiding weaknesses.

Source: *Essential Director*, R.I. (Bob) Tricker, The Economist/Profile Books

Business cycles

The National Bureau of Economic Research has a dating procedure for US business cycles which relies on income, employment, industrial production and wholesale/retail sales as well as GDP growth. The ten-year expansion from March 1991 to March 2001 was the longest in the 150 years covered by the bureau's data.

America's business cycle dates, duration in months

Peak	Trough	Peak to trough	Trough to peak	Trough to trough	Peak to peak
Feb-45	Oct-45	8	80	88	93
Nov-48	Oct-49	11	37	48	45
Jul-53	May-54	10	45	55	56
Aug-57	Apr-58	8	39	47	49
Apr-60	Feb-61	10	24	34	32
Dec-69	Nov-70	11	106	117	116
Nov-73	Mar-75	16	36	52	47
Jan-80	Jul-80	6	58	64	74
Jul-81	Nov-82	16	12	28	18
Jul-90	Mar-91	8	92	100	108
Mar-01	Nov-01	8	120	128	128

Source: National Bureau of Economic Research

The Economic Cycle Research Institute in New York covers data for 20 countries from 1948. It shows that:

The UK rose from a trough in August 1952 to a peak in September 1974, fell briefly to a trough 11 months later, then there was a peak in June 1979, a trough in May 1981, a long expansion to a peak in May 1990 and a short fall to a trough in March 1992.

Japan had a long expansion period from December 1954 to November 1973, then contracted until February 1975 and had another long period of growth until April 1992. A trough in February 1994 followed, then a short rise to a peak in March 1997, a fall until July 1999 and a rise to a peak in August 2000.

Business start-ups and *failures*

United States

	Start-ups, '000	Shut-downs, '000
1990	585	531
1991	541	547
1992	545	522
1993	565	493
1994	571	504
1995	594	497
1996	598	512
1997	591	530
1998	590	541
1999	580	544
2000	574	543
2001	585	553
2002	570	587

Note: Years are to end March.

Source: Office of Advocacy, US Small Business Administration

United Kingdom

	VAT registrations, '000	VAT deregistrations, '000
1994	169.2	174.8
1995	164.9	160.6
1996	169.6	151.5
1997	186.0	148.2
1998	184.8	149.1
1999	178.5	153.4
2000	179.6	156.4
2001	168.4	152.8
2002	175.7	163.9
2003	189.9	174.4

Notes: Value-added tax threshold at the end of 2003 was an annual turnover of £56,000; 1.8m of the estimated 4m enterprises in the UK were VAT-registered.

Source: National Statistics, Small Business Service

Days and procedures to start a business

	Duration of each procedure, days	No. of procedures to register firm		Duration of each procedure, days	No. of procedures to register firm
Albania	47	11	Egypt	43	13
Algeria	26	14	El Salvador	115	12
Angola	146	14	Estonia	72	6
Argentina	32	15	Ethiopia	32	7
Armenia	25	10	Finland	14	3
Australia	2	2	France	8	7
Austria	29	9	Georgia	25	9
Azerbaijan	123	14	Germany	45	9
Bangladesh	35	8	Ghana	85	12
Belarus	79	16	Greece	38	15
Belgium	34	4	Guatemala	39	15
Benin	32	8	Guinea	49	13
Bolivia	59	15	Haiti	203	12
Bosnia	54	12	Honduras	62	13
Botswana	108	11	Hong Kong	11	5
Brazil	152	17	Hungary	52	6
Bulgaria	32	10	India	89	11
Burkina Faso	45	12	Indonesia	151	12
Burundi	43	11	Iran	48	9
Cambodia	94	11	Ireland	24	4
Cameroon	37	12	Israel	34	5
Canada	3	2	Italy	13	9
Central African Rep.	14	10	Jamaica	31	7
Chad	75	19	Japan	31	11
Chile	27	9	Jordan	36	11
China	41	12	Kazakhstan	25	9
Colombia	43	14	Kenya	47	12
Congo-Brazzaville	67	8	Kuwait	35	13
Congo-Kinshasa	155	13	Kirgizstan	21	8
Costa Rica	77	11	Laos	198	9
Cote d'Ivoire	58	11	Latvia	18	7
Croatia	49	12	Lebanon	46	6
Czech Republic	40	10	Lesotho	92	9
Denmark	4	4	Lithuania	26	8
Dominican Republic	78	10	Macedonia	48	13
Ecuador	92	14	Madagascar	44	13

	Duration of each procedure, days	No. of procedures to register firm		Duration of each procedure, days	No. of procedures to register firm
Malawi	35	10	Slovenia	61	10
Malaysia	30	9	South Korea	22	12
Mali	42	13	Spain	108	6
Mexico	58	8	Sri Lanka	50	8
Moldova	30	10	Sweden	16	3
Mongolia	20	8	Switzerland	20	6
Morocco	11	5	Syria	47	12
Mozambique	153	14	Taiwan	48	8
Namibia	85	10	Tanzania	35	13
Netherlands	11	7	Thailand	33	8
New Zealand	12	2	Tunisia	14	9
Nicaragua	45	9	Turkey	9	8
Niger	27	11	Uganda	36	17
Nigeria	44	10	Ukraine	34	15
Norway	23	4	United Arab Emirates	54	12
Oman	34	9	UK	18	6
Pakistan	24	11	US	5	5
Panama	19	7	Uruguay	45	11
Paraguay	74	17	Uzbekistan	35	9
Peru	98	10	Venezuela	116	13
Philippines	50	11	Vietnam	56	11
Poland	31	10	Yemen	63	12
Portugal	78	11	Zambia	35	6
Romania	28	5	Zimbabwe	96	10
Russia	36	9			
Rwanda	21	9	Latin America & Caribbean	70	11
Saudi Arabia	64	12	Sub-Saharan Africa	60	11
Senegal	57	9	East Asia & Pacific	51	8
Serbia & Montenegro	51	11	South Asia	46	9
Sierra Leone	26	9	Europe & Central Asia	42	9
Singapore	8	7	Middle East & North Africa	39	10
Slovakia	52	9	OECD: High income	25	6

Source: World Bank report, January 2004

Corruption: business perceptions

2004, 10=least corrupt

Bangladesh	1.5	Eritrea	2.6
Haiti	1.5	Papua New Guinea	2.6
Nigeria	1.6	Philippines	2.6
Chad	1.7	Uganda	2.6
Myanmar	1.7	Vietnam	2.6
Azerbaijan	1.9	Zambia	2.6
Paraguay	1.9	Algeria	2.7
Angola	2.0	Lebanon	2.7
Congo	2.0	Macedonia	2.7
Côte d'Ivoire	2.0	Nicaragua	2.7
Georgia	2.0	Serbia	2.7
Indonesia	2.0	The Gambia	2.8
Tajikistan	2.0	India	2.8
Turkmenistan	2.0	Malawi	2.8
Cameroon	2.1	Mozambique	2.8
Iraq	2.1	Nepal	2.8
Kenya	2.1	Russia	2.8
Pakistan	2.1	Tanzania	2.8
Bolivia	2.2	Dominican Republic	2.9
Guatemala	2.2	Iran	2.9
Kazakhstan	2.2	Romania	2.9
Kirgizstan	2.2	Mongolia	3.0
Niger	2.2	Senegal	3.0
Sudan	2.2	Armenia	3.1
Ukraine	2.2	Bosnia	3.1
Congo-Brazzaville	2.3	Madagascar	3.1
Ethiopia	2.3	Benin	3.2
Honduras	2.3	Egypt	3.2
Moldova	2.3	Mali	3.2
Sierra Leone	2.3	Morocco	3.2
Uzbekistan	2.3	Turkey	3.2
Venezuela	2.3	Belarus	3.3
Zimbabwe	2.3	Gabon	3.3
Ecuador	2.4	Jamaica	3.3
Yemen	2.4	China	3.4
Albania	2.5	Saudi Arabia	3.4
Argentina	2.5	Syria	3.4
Libya	2.5	Croatia	3.5

Peru	3.5	Botswana	6.0
Poland	3.5	Estonia	6.0
Sri Lanka	3.5	Slovenia	6.0
Ghana	3.6	Oman	6.1
Mexico	3.6	United Arab Emirates	6.1
Thailand	3.6	Uruguay	6.2
Cuba	3.7	Portugal	6.3
Panama	3.7	Israel	6.4
Colombia	3.8	Malta	6.8
Brazil	3.9	Japan	6.9
Latvia	4.0	France	7.1
Slovakia	4.0	Spain	7.1
Bulgaria	4.1	Barbados	7.3
Mauritius	4.1	Chile	7.4
Namibia	4.1	Belgium	7.5
Czech Republic	4.2	Ireland	7.5
El Salvador	4.2	US	7.5
Trinidad & Tobago	4.2	Hong Kong	8.0
Greece	4.3	Germany	8.2
Suriname	4.3	Austria	8.4
South Korea	4.5	Luxembourg	8.4
Kuwait	4.6	Canada	8.5
Lithuania	4.6	UK	8.6
South Africa	4.6	Netherlands	8.7
Hungary	4.8	Australia	8.8
Italy	4.8	Norway	8.9
Costa Rica	4.9	Switzerland	9.1
Malaysia	5.0	Sweden	9.2
Tunisia	5.0	Singapore	9.3
Qatar	5.2	Denmark	9.5
Jordan	5.3	Iceland	9.5
Cyprus	5.4	New Zealand	9.6
Taiwan	5.6	Finland	9.7
Bahrain	5.8		

Corruption: business perceptions

Note: This index ranks countries based on how much corruption is perceived by business people, academics and risk analysts to exist among politicians and public officials.
Source: Transparency International

Business : ratios

These are ratios commonly used in corporate financial analysis.

Working capital

Working capital ratio = current assets/current liabilities, where current assets = stock + debtors + cash at bank and in hand + quoted investments, etc, current liabilities = creditors + overdraft at bank + taxation + dividends, etc. The ratio varies according to type of trade and conditions; a ratio from 1 to 3 is usual, with a ratio above 2 taken to be safe.

Liquidity ratio = liquid ("quick") assets/current liabilities, where liquid assets = debtors + cash at bank and in hand + quoted investments (that is, assets which can be realised within a month or so, which may not apply to all investments); current liabilities are those which may need to be repaid within the same short period, which may not necessarily include a bank overdraft where it is likely to be renewed. The liquidity ratio is sometimes referred to as the "acid test"; a ratio under 1 suggests a possibly difficult situation, while too high a ratio may mean that assets are not being usefully employed.

Turnover of working capital = sales/average working capital. The ratio varies according to type of trade; generally a low ratio can mean poor use of resources, while too high a ratio can mean over-trading. Average working capital or average stock is found by taking the opening and closing working capital or stock and dividing by 2.

Turnover of stock = sales/average stock, or (where cost of sales is known) cost of sales/average stock. The cost of sales turnover figure is to be preferred as both figures are then on the same valuation basis. This ratio can be expressed as number of times per year, or time taken for stock to be turned over once = (52/number of times) weeks. A low turnover of stock can be a sign of stocks that are difficult to move, and usually indicates adverse conditions.

Turnover of debtors = sales/average debtors. This indicates efficiency in collecting accounts. An average credit period of about one month is usual, but varies according to credit stringency conditions in the economy.

Turnover of creditors = purchases/average creditors. Average payment period is best maintained in line with turnover of debtors.

Sales

Export ratio = exports as a percentage of sales.

Sales per employee = sales/average number of employees.

Assets

Ratios of assets can vary according to the measure of assets used:

Total assets = current assets + fixed assets + other assets, where fixed assets = property + plant and machinery + motor vehicles, etc, and other assets = long-term investment + goodwill, etc.

Net assets ("net worth") = total assets – total liabilities = share capital + reserves

Turnover of net assets = sales/average net assets. As for turnover of working capital, a low ratio can mean poor use of resources.

Assets per employee = assets/average number of employees. This indicates the amount of investment backing for employees.

Profits

Profit margin = (profit/sales) × 100 = profits as a percentage of sales; usually profits before tax.

Profitability = (profit/total assets) × 100 = profits as a percentage of total assets.

Return on capital = (profit/net assets) × 100 = profits as a percentage of net assets ("net worth" or "capital employed").

Profit per employee = profit/average number of employees.

Earnings per share (eps) = after-tax profit – minorities/average number of shares in issue.

Busine$$ costs

2004	US=100
Japan	123.8
Germany	113.9
Netherlands	104.0
Iceland	103.3
US	100.0
France	99.1
Luxembourg	99.1
Italy	98.7
UK	97.6
Australia	91.5
Canada	91.0

Note: Based on 12 industries and 27 cost components.
Sources: KPMG, www.competitivealternatives.com

Office occupancy costs, total annual rent, taxes and operating expenses

Jan 2005	$ per sq. metre per year
London (West End)	2,062
Tokyo (Inner Central)	1,339
Paris	1,038
Moscow	753
Frankfurt	676
Hong Kong	634
Mumbai	568
New York (Midtown)	565
Sydney	540
Mexico City	379
Beijing	366
Singapore	345
Istanbul	259
Buenos Aires	253
Bangkok	169

Source: Richard Ellis

Breaking dwn the workforce

2003, m	Canada	Germany	Italy	Japan	UK	US
Professional, technical and related workers	1.4	2.4	0.8	9.1	4.0	26.4
Administrative and managerial workers	2.5	4.9	2.3	1.9	3.3	20.6
Clerical and related workers	2.1	7.4	3.8	12.3	3.7	18.2
Sales workers	2.2	4.4	2.9	9.2	3.6	16.3
Service workers	2.4	4.3	3.6	7.3	4.3	19.2
Agriculture, animal husbandry and forestry workers, fishermen and hunters	0.4	0.7	0.6	2.9	3.3	3.5
Production and related workers, transport equipment operators and labourers	4.8	11.2	7.7	20.6	5.4	32.4
Total	15.7	36.2	22.1	63.2	27.8	136.5

2003, %	Canada	Germany	Italy	Japan	UK	US
Professional, technical and related workers	8.9	6.7	3.4	14.3	14.4	19.4
Administrative and managerial workers	15.6	13.7	10.2	2.9	12.0	15.1
Clerical and related workers	13.4	20.3	17.4	19.5	13.5	13.3
Sales workers	13.8	12.3	13.3	14.5	13.0	11.9
Service workers	15.0	11.9	16.3	11.5	15.4	14.1
Agriculture, animal husbandry and forestry workers, fishermen and hunters	2.6	2.0	2.9	4.6	11.8	2.5
Production and related workers, transport equipment operators and labourers	30.6	31.0	34.9	32.6	19.4	23.7

Note: Data for France are unavailable and data for the US are for 2002; totals may not always add to 100 due to rounding, and exclusion of small numbers of "Other" for some countries.
Source: International Labour Organisation

The changing workforce

Numbers of workers, m

	Canada	France	Germany	Italy	Japan	UK	US
1970	8.7	21.6	35.4	21.1	53.3	25.6	87.3
1975	10.5	22.9	36.8	21.9	56.0	26.4	98.3
1980	12.2	23.8	37.5	22.6	57.2	26.9	110.1
1985	13.3	24.2	38.1	23.5	60.9	27.6	117.6
1990	14.7	24.7	39.9	24.4	64.1	28.6	125.7
1995	15.6	25.7	40.9	25.3	67.0	29.0	134.2
2000	16.5	26.7	40.9	25.7	68.3	29.5	145.1
2003	16.9	27.1	41.2	25.6	67.9	29.6	149.8

Unemployment trends, % of labour force

	Canada	France	Germany	Italy	Japan	UK	US
1980	7.5	6.1	…	7.6	2.0	6.8	7.1
1981	7.6	7.0	…	7.9	2.3	10.4	7.6
1982	11.0	7.8	…	8.5	2.3	10.9	9.7
1983	11.9	8.0	…	9.4	2.7	11.7	9.6
1984	11.3	9.5	…	10.1	2.7	11.8	7.5
1985	10.7	10.2	…	10.3	2.6	11.3	7.2
1986	9.6	10.1	…	11.2	2.8	11.2	7.0
1987	8.8	10.6	…	12.0	2.9	10.8	6.2
1988	7.8	10.1	…	12.1	2.5	8.8	5.5
1989	7.5	9.5	…	12.1	2.2	7.2	5.3
1990	8.1	9.2	…	11.4	2.1	6.8	5.6
1991	10.3	9.0	6.6	11.0	2.1	8.4	6.8
1992	11.2	10.0	7.9	11.6	2.2	9.7	7.5
1993	11.4	11.1	9.5	10.0	2.5	10.3	6.9
1994	10.4	12.3	10.3	11.0	2.9	9.6	6.1
1995	9.4	11.6	10.1	11.4	3.2	8.6	5.6
1996	9.6	12.1	8.8	11.5	3.4	8.2	5.4
1997	9.1	12.3	9.8	11.6	3.4	7.1	4.9
1998	8.3	11.8	9.7	11.6	4.1	6.1	4.5
1999	7.6	11.7	8.8	11.3	4.7	6.0	4.2
2000	6.8	10.0	7.9	10.5	4.8	5.5	4.0
2001	7.2	8.8	7.9	9.5	5.0	4.8	4.7
2002	7.7	8.9	8.7	9.0	5.4	5.1	5.8
2003	7.6	9.7	10.0	8.7	5.3	4.8	6.0

Source International Labour Organisation

The sex divide

	Male, m	Female, m	Male, %	Female, %
Canada				
1985*	6.76	4.98	57.61	42.39
2003	8.41	7.34	53.39	46.61
% change			-7.32	9.94
France				
1973	13.43	7.73	63.46	36.54
2001†	13.15	10.96	54.67	45.33
% change			-13.85	24.04
Germany				
1991*	21.88	15.57	58.42	41.58
2003	20.00	16.18	55.28	44.72
% change			-5.37	7.55
Italy				
1973	13.81	5.34	72.12	27.88
2003	13.77	8.37	62.21	37.79
% change			-13.74	35.55
Japan				
1973	32.35	20.23	61.51	38.47
2003	37.19	25.97	58.88	41.12
% change			-4.28	6.89
UK				
1973	13.77	8.89	60.77	39.23
2003	13.14	12.86	50.55	49.45
% change			-16.82	26.06
US				
1973	52.35	32.72	61.54	38.46
2003	73.33	64.40	53.24	46.76
% change			-13.49	21.58

* First year available.
† Last year available.
Source: International Labour Organisation

Changes in working hours

Average annual hours worked per employed person

	1950	2003
Australia	1,838	1,814
Austria	1,976	1,550
Belgium	2,283	1,542
Canada	1,967	1,718
Denmark	2,283	1,475
Finland	2,035	1,713
France	1,926	1,453
Germany	2,316	1,429
Ireland	2,250	1,613
Italy	1,997	1,591
Japan	2,166	1,801
Netherlands	2,208	1,345
Norway	2,101	1,337
Spain	2,200	1,800
Sweden	1,951	1,564
UK	1,958	1,673
US	1,867	1,792

Source: OECD

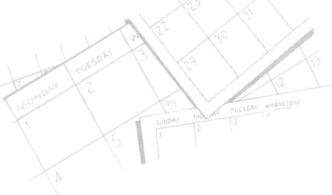

Changes in retirement **age**

	Men		Women	
	1969	2003	1969	2003
Australia	65	65	60	62.5
Austria	65	65	60	60
Belgium	65	65	60	63
Canada	66	65	66	65
Denmark	67	65	67	65
Finland	65	65	65	65
France	65	60	65	60
Germany	65	65	65	65
Greece	60	65	55	65
Ireland	70	66	70	66
Italy	60	65	55	65
Japan	65	65	65	65
Luxembourg	65	65	62	65
Netherlands	65	65	65	65
Norway	70	67	70	67
New Zealand	65	65	65	65
Portugal	65	65	65	65
Spain	65	65	55	65
Sweden	67	65	67	65
Switzerland	65	65	62	63
Turkey	65	60	55	55
UK	65	65	60	60
US	65	65	65	65

Source: OECD

Days lost in strikes and lock outs

Man days, m

	Canada	France	Germany	Italy	Japan	UK	US
1971	2.87	4.39	na	14.80	6.03	13.55	47.59
1972	7.75	3.76	na	19.50	5.15	23.91	27.07
1973	5.78	3.91	na	23.42	4.60	7.20	27.95
1974	9.22	3.38	na	19.47	9.66	14.75	31.81
1975	10.91	3.87	na	27.19	8.02	6.01	17.56
1976	11.61	4.05	na	25.38	3.25	3.28	23.96
1977	3.31	2.43	na	16.57	1.52	10.14	21.26
1978	7.39	2.08	na	10.18	1.36	9.41	23.77
1979	7.83	3.17	na	27.53	0.93	29.47	20.41
1980	8.98	1.52	na	16.46	1.00	11.96	20.84
1981	8.88	1.44	na	10.53	0.55	4.27	16.91
1982	5.80	2.25	na	18.56	0.54	5.31	9.06
1983	4.44	1.32	na	14.00	0.51	3.75	17.46
1984	3.88	1.32	na	8.70	0.35	27.14	8.50
1985	3.13	0.73	na	3.83	0.26	6.40	7.08
1986	7.15	0.57	na	5.64	0.25	1.92	11.86
1987	3.81	0.51	na	4.61	0.26	3.55	4.47
1988	4.90	1.09	na	3.32	0.17	3.70	4.38
1989	3.70	0.80	na	4.44	0.22	4.13	16.53
1990	5.08	0.53	na	5.18	0.14	1.90	5.93
1991	2.52	0.50	na	2.99	0.10	0.76	4.58
1992	2.11	0.36	na	2.74	0.23	0.53	3.99
1993	1.52	0.51	0.59	3.41	0.12	0.65	3.98
1994	1.61	0.50	0.23	3.37	0.09	0.28	5.02
1995	1.58	0.78	0.25	0.91	0.08	0.42	5.77
1996	3.35	0.44	0.10	1.93	0.04	1.30	4.89
1997	3.61	0.39	0.05	1.16	0.11	0.23	4.50
1998	2.44	0.35	0.02	0.58	0.10	0.28	5.12
1999	2.45	0.57	0.08	0.91	0.09	0.24	2.00
2000	1.66	0.81	0.01	0.88	0.04	0.50	20.42
2001	2.20	0.69	0.03	1.03	0.03	0.53	1.15
2002	3.03	na	0.31	4.86	0.01	1.32	0.66
2003	1.74	na	0.16	1.96	na	0.50	4.08

Source: International Labour Organisation

Labour union **strength** 🚶🚶🚶🚶🚶🚶🚶🚶🚶🚶🚶🚶🚶

Latest year

	Union members, m	% of workforce
Australia	1.9	23
Belgium	2.7	58
Brazil	17.4	44
Canada	3.6	30
China	134.0	90
Colombia	1.1	29
Denmark	2.1	87
Finland	2.2	100
France	6.0	31
Germany	8.3	26
Hong Kong	0.7	21
Iceland	0.1	92
India	6.4	na
Ireland	0.5	39
Japan	10.5	20
Malaysia	0.8	na
Netherlands	1.9	27
New Zealand	0.3	18
Norway	1.5	72
Pakistan	0.4	na
Philippines	3.9	27
Singapore	0.4	22
Slovakia	0.7	39
South Africa	2.5	58
South Korea	1.6	12
Sweden	3.7	98
Switzerland	0.8	26
Taiwan	2.9	38
Turkey	2.6	58
UK	6.8	29
US	15.8	13

Source: International Labour Organisation

Labour union federations

	Union federation	Members, m
Austria	Austrian Federation of Trade Unions (OeGB)	1.4
Belgium	Confederation of Christian Trade Unions (CSC)	1.6
Brazil	Workers' Single Headquarters (CUT)	22.5
Canada	Canadian Union of Public Employees (CUPE)	0.5
China	All-China Federation of Trade Unions (ACFTU)	134.0
Czech Republic	Czech-Moravian Confederation of Trade Unions (CMKOS)	1.0
Denmark	Danish Federation of Trade Unions (LO)	1.2
Finland	Central Organisation of Finnish Trade Unions (SAK)	1.0
France	French Democratic Confederation of Labour (CFDT)	0.8
Germany	German Federation of Trade Unions (DGB)	7.7
Greece	Greek Federation of Labour (GSEE)	0.5
Hungary	Confederation of Hungarian Trade Unions (MSZOSZ)	0.2
India	Indian National Trade Union Congress (INTUC)	6.0
Ireland	Irish Congress of Trade Unions (ICTU)	0.7
Italy	Italian General Confederation of Labour (CGIL)	5.5
Japan	National Confederation of Trade Unions (Zenroren)	1.5
Mexico	Workers' Congress (CT)	12.5
Netherlands	Dutch Trade Union Federation (FNV)	1.2
Norway	Norwegian Confederation of Trade Unions (LO)	0.8
Poland	Solidarity (NSZZ)	1.2
Portugal	General Confederation of Portuguese Workers (CGTP)	0.7
Russia	Federation of Independent Trade Unions of Russia (FNPR)	28.0
Slovakia	Confederation of Trade Unions of the Slovak Republic (KOZ SR)	0.6
South Africa	Congress of South African Trade Unions (COSATU)	2+
South Korea	Korean Confederation of Trade Unions (KCTU)	0.6
Spain	Trade Union Confederation of Workers' Commissions (CCOO)	1.0
Sweden	Swedish Trade Union Confederation (LO)	1.9
Switzerland	Swiss Federation of Trade Unions (SGB/USS)	0.4
UK	Trades Union Congress (TUC)	6.5
US	AFL-CIO	13.0

Sources: Union federations; www.fedee.com/tradeunions.html

Big unions

	Union	Trade	Members, m
Canada	Canadian Union of Public Employees (CUPE)	Public services	0.5
France	French Democratic Confederation of Labour (CFDT)	Diversified	0.8
Germany	IG Metall	Industry	2.4
Italy	Italian General Confederation of Labour (CGIL)	Diversified	5.5
Japan	All Japan Prefectural and Municipal Workers' Union (JICHIRO)	Public services	0.9
UK	UNISON	Public services	1.3
US	American Federation of State, County and Municipal Employees (AFSCME)	Public services	1.4
US	Teamsters (IBOT)	Diversified	1.4

Sources: Unions; www.fedee.com/tradeunions.html

International pay comparisons

Gross salary $000, 2003	Labourer (general)	Labourer (skilled)	Professional (junior)	Professional (senior)	Management (lower middle)	Management (upper middle)
Australia	26.2	31.8	39.5	51.0	67.9	91.9
Austria	24.1	33.2	45.8	63.1	86.9	119.7
Belgium	33.8	40.9	49.6	63.0	83.7	111.1
Brazil	5.6	9.0	14.4	23.2	36.3	60.3
Bulgaria	3.7	5.5	8.1	13.2	19.9	29.9
Canada	31.4	37.6	45.5	58.4	61.2	74.3
China	2.5	5.2	8.0	14.7	25.8	45.8
Czech Republic	6.1	9.4	14.5	22.5	34.8	53.9
Denmark	30.3	39.9	52.5	69.1	91.0	119.7
France	22.7	30.0	39.6	52.2	68.9	90.9
Germany	34.2	45.2	59.7	78.9	104.3	137.8
Hong Kong	20.8	29.4	41.5	58.7	83.0	117.4
Hungary	7.1	10.7	15.9	24.3	37.4	46.5
India	3.1	4.9	7.9	12.5	20.0	31.9
Indonesia	2.6	4.5	7.7	13.2	22.6	38.6
Ireland	33.0	41.1	51.3	64.0	79.9	99.6
Italy	17.4	24.6	34.9	49.4	70.0	99.2
Japan	40.1	49.8	61.9	77.0	95.7	118.9
Malaysia	5.7	8.3	12.0	17.2	24.9	35.9
Mexico	9.8	14.8	22.4	33.9	59.0	92.5
Netherlands	29.3	38.0	49.4	64.3	83.6	111.5
New Zealand	20.2	28.1	35.3	43.8	56.2	75.0
Norway	27.8	35.4	44.9	57.0	72.5	92.0
Poland	6.5	10.0	15.2	23.1	35.2	53.6
Portugal	14.6	20.6	28.9	40.7	57.3	80.6
Romania	1.9	3.5	6.3	11.5	20.9	37.8
Singapore	13.6	19.3	27.3	38.8	55.1	78.1
South Korea	17.3	22.7	29.9	39.3	51.8	68.2
Spain	21.9	29.0	38.5	51.0	67.5	89.4
Sweden	27.4	32.6	38.9	46.2	59.2	79.4
Switzerland	43.1	57.0	75.5	99.8	132.1	174.8
Taiwan	13.4	19.0	26.8	37.9	53.7	76.0
Thailand	4.3	6.9	11.1	17.7	28.4	45.5
Turkey	8.6	13.7	21.8	34.8	55.5	88.4
UK	20.5	28.3	39.0	53.9	74.4	102.7
US	18.2	26.9	39.9	59.2	87.7	130.0

Source: Mercer

Average earning$ and the minimum wage

2002	Average wage, $*	Statutory minimum wage, $	Minimum wage as % of average wage
Australia	27,708	12,798	46
Belgium	28,917	13,176	46
Canada	25,322	9,269	37
Czech Republic	6,415	2,126	33
France	20,749	12,919	62
Greece	10,758	5,438	51
Hungary	4,219	2,348	56
Ireland	24,053	11,918	50
Japan	33,843	10,987	32
South Korea	18,734	4,662	25
Luxembourg	29,605	14,767	50
New Zealand	19,613	8,177	42
Poland	6,548	2,266	35
Portugal	7,940	3,943	50
Slovakia	2,912	1,279	44
Spain	15,445	5,768	37
UK	28,577	12,640	44
US	32,360	10,712	33

*Average annual wage is for a full-time production worker.
Source: OECD Tax-Benefit Models and Minimum Wage Database 2004

US chief executive pay

2004	Company	Total compensation, $m
Terry Semel	Yahoo!	230.55
Barry Diller	InterActiveCorp	156.17
William McGuire	UnitedHealth Group	124.77
Howard Solomon	Forest Laboratories	92.12
George David	United Technologies	88.71
Lew Frankfort	Coach	86.48
Edwin Crawford	Caremark Rx	77.86
Ray Irani	Occidental Petroleum	64.14
Angelo Mozilo	Countrywide Financial	56.96
Richard Fairbank	Capital One Financial	56.66
John Wilder	TXU	54.87
Richard Kovacevich	Wells Fargo	53.08
Robert Toll	Toll Brothers	50.24
Lawrence Ellison	Oracle	45.80
William Greehey	Valero Energy	44.88
Irwin Jacobs	Qualcomm	44.42
Rodney Mott	Intl Steel Group	42.75
John Chambers	Cisco Systems	40.18
Richard Fuld	Lehman Brothers Holdings	40.13
Bruce Karatz	KB Home	38.82
Jerry Grundhofer	US Bancorp	38.58
Kevin Rollins	Dell	38.47
Bob Simpson	XTO Energy	38.34
Dwight Schar	NVR	38.23
James Tobin	Boston Scientific	38.15
Raymond Gilmartin	Merck & Co	37.79
Frederick Smith	FedEx	36.41
Larry Mizel	MDC Holdings	34.56

Source: *Forbes*

UK chief executive pay

2004	Company	Pay, £m	Pension pot, £m
Michael Davis	Xstrata	4.69	na
Stanley Fink	Man Group	3.81	na
Micky Arison*	Carnival	3.76	0.5
Lord Browne of Madingley	BP	3.74	15.2
Bart Becht	Reckitt Benkiser	3.63	na
Sir Terry Leahy	Tesco	3.19	3.8
Sir Fred Goodwin	Royal Bank of Scotland	2.52	3.59
Arun Sarin	Vodafone	2.51	na
J. P. Garnier	GlaxoSmithKline	2.47	6.29
Gareth Davis	Imperial Tobacco	2.46	5.61
Martin Sorrell	WPP	2.42	na
Tom Glocer	Reuters	2.32	na
Niall FitzGerald*	Unilever	2.32	16.9
Charles Goodyear	BHP Billiton	2.29	na
Francesco Caio	Cable & Wireless	2.19	na
Philip Bowman	Allied Domecq	2.19	na
Paul Walsh	Diageo	2.18	6.53
Mervyn Davies	Standard Chartered	2.17	1.98
Todd Sitzer	Cadbury Schweppes	2.15	3.14
Stuart Rose	Marks & Spencer	2.12	na
John Varley	Barclays	2.07	4.7
Michael Dobson	Schroders	2.01	0.09
Keith Butler-Wheelhouse	Smiths Group	1.97	na
Ben Verwaayen	BT	1.97	na
Crispin Davis	Reed Elsevier	1.95	3.96
Charlie Banks	Wolseley	1.91	na
Eric Daniels	Lloyds TSB	1.90	1.14
Charles Allen	ITV	1.88	6.57

*Chief executive and chairman.
Source: *Daily Telegraph*

The number of acc%untants

2001	Public practice	Business	Government	Total	No. of accountants as % of pop.
Austria	8,076	na	na	8,076	0.100
Belgium	4,659	2,329	na	6,988	0.068
Czech Republic	1,314	308	na	1,622	0.016
Denmark	1,903	785	20	2,708	0.050
Finland	1,436	62	19	1,517	0.029
France	29,614	na	na	29,614	0.050
Germany	9,047	na	na	9,047	0.011
Greece	505	na	na	505	0.005
Hungary	3,611	1,168	584	5,363	0.054
Ireland	4,675	13,280	219	18,174	0.466
Italy	88,350	1,470	980	90,800	0.158
Luxembourg	606	10	2	618	0.155
Malta	482	424	31	937	0.234
Netherlands	4,521	5,386	1,279	11,186	0.069
Norway	2,800	190	50	3,040	0.068
Poland	7,723	na	na	7,723	0.020
Portugal	899	na	na	899	0.009
Romania	9,017	na	13	9,030	0.040
Slovenia	270	177	24	471	0.024
Spain	2,829	2,447	na	5,276	0.013
Sweden	2,030	na	13	2,043	0.023
Switzerland	3,500	100	100	3,700	0.051
UK	83,948	175,178	25,003	284,129	0.481
US	na	na	na	600000*	0.206

*Estimate

Sources: The Federation of European Accountants; National Association of State Boards of Accountancy; UNDP, HDR

Leading acc%unting firms

2004	KPMG	Pricewaterhouse-Coopers	Ernst & Young	Deloitte & Touche
Country presence	148	144	140	148
Partners	6,448	7,753	na	na
Client service professionals	70,095	88,471	77,043	na
Administration and support staff	17,440	26,247	23,558	na
Total employees	93,983	122,471	100,601	117,000
Global revenue, $bn	13	16	15	16

Revenue by geographic breakdown, $bn

2004	KPMG	Pricewaterhouse-Coopers	Ernst & Young	Deloitte & Touche
Americas	4.93	6.33	6.36	8.20
Asia Pacific	1.67	2.21*	1.66	6.60
Europe, Middle East, South Asia, and Africa	6.84	7.71†	6.53	1.60

*Includes Asia, Australasia and Pacific Islands. †Excludes South Asia

Revenue by functional breakdown, $bn

2004	KPMG	Pricewaterhouse-Coopers	Ernst & Young	Deloitte & Touche
Audit	6.42	8.71*	9.03	7.40
Tax	3.11	4.46	4.26	3.80
Advisory Services	3.91	3.08	1.09	1.20
Consulting	na	na	na	4.00
Other	na	na	0.17	na

*Assurance

People by geographic breakdown

2004	KPMG	Pricewaterhouse-Coopers	Ernst & Young	Deloitte & Touche
Americas	na	na	33,549	50,500
Asia Pacific	na	na	22,507	20,000
Europe, Middle East, South Asia, Africa	na	na	44,545	46,500

Source: Company reports

A world of lawyers

2004	No. of lawyers	No. of lawyers as % of population
Belgium	13,050	0.125
Czech Republic	6,000	0.059
Denmark	4,300	0.080
Egypt	2,000	0.003
England & Wales	121,165	0.230
Finland	1,600	0.031
France	36,000	0.059
Germany	116,000	0.141
Greece	25,000	0.234
Hungary	8,000	0.078
Ireland	7,900	0.203
Israel	27,000	0.409
Italy	70,000	0.121
Netherlands	11,200	0.070
Norway	5,600	0.124
Portugal	23,000	0.225
Romania	13,000	0.058
Russia	19,000	0.013
Scotland	9,443	0.190
Spain	104,000	0.244
Sweden	4,100	0.046
Switzerland	7,000	0.095
US*	1,084,504	0.366

*As of December 31st 2003.

Sources: American Bar Association; Legal 500; US Census Bureau; The Law Society of England & Wales; The Law Society of Scotland; National Statistics UK

Leading law firms

2004	Gross revenue, £m	Lawyers, total	Partners	Equity partners	Location
Clifford Chance	950.0	2,684	626	406	UK
Skadden Arps Slate Meagher & Flom	813.9	1,650	350	350	US
Freshfields Bruckhaus Deringer	785.0	2,225	516	516	UK
Linklaters	720.0	2,000	470	390	UK
Baker & McKenzie	694.0	3,053	611	611	US
Allen & Overy	652.0	1,879	431	312	UK
Jones Day	633.4	1,970	601	427	US
Latham & Watkins	632.2	1,513	444	367	US
Sidley Austin Brown & Wood	566.7	1,421	562	288	US
Mayer Brown Rowe & Maw	497.5	1,249	472	426	US
White & Case	496.3	1,552	325	238	US
Weil Gotshal & Manges	490.2	1,015	251	181	US
Shearman & Sterling	447.0	988	231	203	US
Kirkland & Ellis	443.7	854	345	157	US
Sullivan & Cromwell	420.4	647	152	152	US
McDermott Will & Emery	408.8	901	537	283	US
O'Melveny & Myers	402.7	909	245	227	US
Gibson Dunn & Crutcher	395.0	747	241	241	US
Morgan Lewis & Bockius	386.1	1,063	363	204	US
Lovells	377.0	1,153	333	255	UK
Davis Polk & Wardwell	359.2	581	146	146	US
Akin Gump Strauss Hauer & Feld	358.0	832	315	214	US
Cleary Gottlieb Steen & Hamilton	354.9	758	161	161	US
Simpson Thacher & Bartlett	352.8	637	145	145	US
Greenberg Traurig	350.3	952	441	231	US

Source: *The Lawyer*

Women in business

Firsts among women

1809 Mary Kies – first woman to receive
a US patent (for weaving straw in hatmaking)

1963 Katharine Graham – first woman CEO in the
Fortune 500 list of US companies (The Washington Post Co)

1967 Muriel "Mickey" Siebert – first woman to purchase a seat on
the New York Stock Exchange

1997 Marjorie Scardino – first woman CEO of a FTSE100
company (Pearson)

1999 Carly Fiorina – first woman CEO in the 30-company Dow
Jones Industrial Average (Hewlett-Packard)

2001 Clara Furse – first woman to become CEO of the London
Stock Exchange

2002 Baroness Sarah Hogg – first chair of a FTSE100 company (3i)

Sources: Press reports

Most powerful women in business in America

Meg Whitman	eBay CEO
Carly Fiorina	Hewlett-Packard CEO (resigned in February 2005)
Andrea Jung	Avon Products CEO
Anne Mulcahy	Xerox CEO
Marjorie Magner	Citigroup CEO of Global Consumer Group
Oprah Winfrey	Harpo chairman
Sallie Krawcheck	Citigroup CFO
Abigail Johnson	Fidelity Management & Research president
Pat Woertz	ChevronTexaco executive vice-president, Global Downstream
Karen Katen	Pfizer executive vice-president; Global Pharmaceuticals president

Source: *Fortune*

Most powerful women outside America

Anne Lauvergeon	Areva	France	Chairman
Xie Qihua	Shanghai Baosteel Group	China	Chairman and president
Marjorie Scardino	Pearson	UK	CEO
Nancy McKinstry	Wolters Kluwer	Netherlands	CEO
Ho Ching	Temasek Holdings	Singapore	Executive director
Ana Patricia Botín	Banco Banesto	Spain	Chairman
Linda Cook	Shell Gas & Power	Netherlands	CEO
Yang Mianmian	Haier Group	China	President
Marina Berlusconi	Fininvest	Italy	Vice-chairman
Kate Swann	WH Smith	UK	CEO

Source: *Fortune*

Most powerful women working in entertainment

Anne Sweeney	The Walt Disney Company	Co-chairman of media networks; president of Disney-ABC Television Group
Amy Pascal	Sony Pictures Entertainment	Vice-chairman
Nancy Tellem	CBS Paramount Network Television Entertainment Group	President
Judy McGrath	MTV Networks	Chairman and CEO
Stacey Snider	Universal Pictures	Chairman
Gail Merman	Fox Broadcasting	President of entertainment
Sherry Lansing	Paramount Motion Picture Group	Chairman
Oprah Winfrey	Buena Vista Motion Pictures Group	President
Dana Walden	20th Century Fox Television	President

Source: *Hollywood Reporter*
Note: Most powerful women rankings are for 2004.

Outsourcing and offshoring

Outsourcing is when a firm subcontracts part of its operations – for example, IT services – to another firm. Offshoring is when the outsourcing is to a firm in another country.

Beginnings and developments The outsourcing business has its origins in manufacturing, especially of electronics, when in the 1980s western (mainly American) companies shifted operations to Latin America, the Caribbean and Asia. In the 1990s, companies began to relocate IT services, which in 2005 accounted for about two-thirds of all outsourcing. At first, Ireland was a favoured destination, but India soon took a lead and in 2004 it was reckoned to account for 80% of the offshore market. However, in the same year Europe accounted for 49% of the value of all new outsourcing contracts worth more than $50m, ahead of the United States (42%), with Germany accounting for 12.5% of the world market. The financial-services industry leads the trend.

America resists the trend With the aim of stopping jobs moving offshore, in 2004, two American states passed laws limiting offshoring, and 16 more states were in 2005 considering similar moves. A survey by Bain in 2005 found increasing dissatisfaction with the quality of outsourced work.

Linguistic factors English-speaking countries enjoy a significant competitive advantage in offshoring, as the business is dominated by American and British companies able to take advantage of flexible laws that allow them (so far) to shift operations abroad, and because English is so widely spoken across the world. India has found itself in a particularly strong position with its large pool of well educated, English-speaking workers.

Competition for offshoring business India faces competition for outsourced jobs from Malaysia, the Philippines and China. But PricewaterhouseCoopers in 2003 estimated the cost of operations in India to be 37% lower than in China and 17% lower than in Malaysia. The Philippines produces 300,000 English-speaking college graduates per year, against India's 2m, 80% of whom speak English.

Rightshoring There has been a huge shift in call-centre services from Britain to India and elsewhere, where call-centre salaries are around ten times lower than in the UK. However, increasing customer dissatisfaction with shifting of services that require local knowledge has led to the growth of "rightshoring" – ie, only relocating those services that can be done effectively offshore.

Cost factors Besides lower wages, the growth in outsourcing has been driven by the drop in the price of telecommunications. A report by HSBC showed an 80% drop in the price of a one-minute telephone call from India to Britain or the United States between 2001 and 2003.

Third party growth In the early 1990s, the offshoring that took place was usually when companies set up their own back-office operations in India. These are gradually being superseded by cheaper third parties, many of which reaped the benefits of work from overloaded western firms during the run-up to Y2K. Gradually, however, cost advantages are eroding as Indian IT salaries grow in response to demand for skills.

Slow down on the horizon As salaries offshore catch up and firms discover that it is not always easy to manage the quality of services provided offshore, offshoring will begin to lose some of its attractions. In America, Citigroup, a bank, hired 100 college students in 2003 for programming work at half the pay it would have needed to pay Indian programmers. Development of speech-recognition software may also eventually lead to a decline in staff-heavy call-centre work in India or anywhere else.

More competition for Bangalore The city of Bangalore has been the hub of India's offshoring and the business process outsourcing (BPO) boom, accounting for more than one-third of Indian employment in IT and BPO. Yet its boom, plus a neglectful government, has led to infrastructure problems, for traffic in particular, and it now faces aggressive competition from many other Indian cities, including Gurgaon and Noida on the edge of Delhi, Chennai (formerly Madras), Hyderabad and Pune.

Sources: *The Economist*; *Offshore Outsourcing* by Marcia Robinson and Ravi Kalakota, Mivar Press

TALL buildings

Office	Height, m	Height, ft	No. of floors	Year completed	Location
Taipei 101	509	1671	101	2004	Taipei
Petronas Tower 1	452	1483	88	1998	Kuala Lumpur
Petronas Tower 2	452	1483	88	1998	Kuala Lumpur
Sears Tower	442	1450	108	1974	Chicago
Two International Finance	415	1362	88	2003	Hong Kong
CITIC Plaza	391	1283	80	1997	Guangzhou
Shun Hing Square	384	1260	69	1996	Shenzhen
Empire State Building	381	1250	102	1931	New York City
Central Plaza	374	1227	78	1992	Hong Kong
Bank of China Tower	367	1205	72	1990	Hong Kong

Residential	Height, m	Height, ft	No. of floors	Year completed	Location
21st Century Tower	269	883	55	2003	Dubai
Triumph-Palace	264	866	54	2004	Moscow
Tower Palace Three Tower	264	865	73	2004	Seoul
Trump World Tower	262	861	72	2001	New York City
Sorrento 1	256	841	75	2003	Hong Kong
Mok-dong Hyperion I Tower	256	840	69	2003	Seoul
The Harbourside	255	837	75	2003	Hong Kong
Highcliff	252	828	72	2003	Hong Kong
State Tower	247	811	68	2001	Bangkok
The Tower	243	796	54	2002	Dubai

Hotels	Height, m	Height, ft	No. of floors	Year completed	Location
Ryugyong Hotel	330	1,083	105	1992	Pyongyang
Burj Al Arab	321	1,053	60	1999	Dubai
Emirates Hotel Tower	309	1,014	56	2000	Dubai
Baiyoke Tower II	304	997	85	1997	Bangkok
JR Central Hotel Tower	226	741	53	2000	Nagoya
Swissôtel The Stamford	226	741	73	1986	Singapore
Marriott Renaissance Centre	221	726	73	1977	Detroit
Westin Peachtree Plaza	220	723	73	1976	Atlanta
Four Seasons Hotel	208	682	52	1993	New York City
Sofitel Jin Jiang Oriental	207	679	46	2002	Shanghai

Note: Burj Dubai will be the tallest building standing at 705m (2313ft) once completed in 2008.
Source: Emporis

BIG shopping malls

US, 2004

	Retail space, sq. feet, m	No. of shops	Location	Year opened
South Coast Plaza	2.700	280	Orange County, California	1967
Sawgrass Mills	2.503	300	Sunrise, Florida	1990
Del Amo Fashion Centre	2.500	300	Torrance, California	1975
Mall of America	2.500	428	Bloomington, Minnesota	1992
Galleria	2.400	375	Dallas, Texas	1970
Woodfield Mall	2.224	245	Chicago, Illinois	1971
Roosevelt Field Mall	2.146	220	Garden City, New York	1956
Millcreek Mall	2.139	171	Erie, Pennsylvania	1974
Lakewood Centre	2.121	255	Lakewood, California	1951
NorthPark Centre	2.100	160	Dallas, Texas	1965
Tysons Corner Centre	2.091	250	Washington, DC	1968
Oakbrook Shopping Centre	2.087	175	Oak Brook, Illinois	1962

Source: Eastern Connecticut State University, Emil Pocock

UK, 2004

	Location	Retail space*, sq. metres, 000
Merry Hill	Brierley Hill	136.18
Bluewater	Kent	122.91
Metro Centre	Gateshead	122.38
Trafford Centre	Manchester	121.64
Lakeside	Essex	112.04
Meadowhall Centre	Sheffield	108.51
Braehead	Renfrew	95.78
Brent Cross	North London	57.72
Cribbs Causeway	Bristol	57.38
Edinburgh – Ocean Terminal	Edinburgh	20.23

*Not including service outlets, leisure facilities, vacants and non-selling space
Source: Experian Business Strategies

Leading headhunters

2004	Revenue, $m	% change 2003–04	Revenue per consultant ($'000)	No. of offices*
Korn/Ferry	402.2†	29.4	1,008.0	73
Heidrick & Struggles	375.4	18.1	1,264.0	58
Spencer Stuart	362.4‡	18.2	1,289.0	49
Egon Zehnder	335.7	23.5	1,180.0	59
Russell Reynolds	268.0	33.0	1,120.0	32
Ray & Berndtson	147.4	16.8	491.3	51
Amrop Hever	135.3	20.3	512.5	79
Globe	76.0	23.0	1,100.0	17
IIC Partners	75.3	11.3	418.3	53
Transearch	70.0	39.4	345.0	53

*2005.
†Year ending October 2004.
‡Year ending September 2004.

Leading lies on CVs

A Korn/Ferry survey (*Executive Recruiter Index*, May 2004) asked headhunters to select three types of information that are most frequently fabricated or obfuscated by candidates. These are:

- reasons for leaving previous job (69%);
- results/accomplishments (68%);
- job responsibilities (45%).

Also mentioned were compensation (39%), education (24%) and dates of employment (20%). The study also looked at what kinds of due diligence clients are asking for in candidate background checks. Education verification (83%), employment verification (77%) and criminal/arrest history (35%) ranked as the top three areas.

Leading advertising firms

Global revenue, 2004, $m

Omnicom Group	US	9,747
WPP Group	UK	9,370
Interpublic Group	US	6,201
Publicis Groupe	France	4,777
Dentsu	Japan	2,851
Havas	France	1,866
Aegis Group	UK	1,374
Hakuhodo DY Holdings	Japan	1,372
Asatsu-DK	Japan	473
Carlson Marketing Group	US	347
MDC Partners	Canada/US	317
Incepta Group	UK	280
Monster Worldwide	US	252
Digitas	US	252
HealthSTAR Communications	US	203
Alloy	US	194
Cheil Communications	South Korea	186
Aspen Marketing Services	US	180
G2R	South Korea	180
Tokyu Agency	Japan	176
George P. Johnson Co	US	173
aQuantive	US	158
Doner	US	156
Clemenger Communications	Australia	147
Select Communications	Germany	145

Source: *Ad Age*

$pending on advertising

	Total, 2004, $m	% of GDP	Per head, 2003, $
Argentina	935	0.64	21.5
Australia	5,972	1.11	275.4
Austria	2,286	0.87	266.6
Belgium	2,625	0.83	236.0
Brazil	4,653	0.80	20.6
Canada	6,381	0.70	193.6
Chile	561	0.72	33.6
China	9,036	0.56	5.9
Colombia	989	1.21	21.7
Czech Republic	1,363	1.43	120.9
Denmark	1,769	0.80	313.6
Estonia	72	0.72	49.6
Finland	1,279	0.76	233.7
France	11,257	0.61	179.1
Germany	18,309	0.74	218.7
Greece	2,748	1.48	228.0
Hong Kong	2,234	1.33	262.0
Hungary	1,963	2.15	167.1
India	2,716	0.41	2.0
Indonesia	2,732	1.18	8.6
Ireland	1,556	0.94	330.9
Israel	757	0.65	110.8
Italy	9,454	0.62	153.8
Japan	37,630	0.85	283.8
Latvia	85	0.67	32.6
Lithuania	109	0.56	24.9
Malaysia	1,164	1.04	40.3
Mexico	3,428	0.53	30.7
Netherlands	3,843	0.73	241.9
New Zealand	1,112	1.30	264.9
Norway	2,358	1.03	480.2
Panama	222	1.61	62.8
Peru	216	0.34	8.7
Philippines	600	0.67	6.6
Poland	3,265	1.41	76.1
Portugal	1,047	0.68	95.1
Puerto Rico	1,891	2.40	448.7
Russia	3,855	0.83	20.2

	Total, 2004, $m	% of GDP	Per head, 2003, $
Saudi Arabia/Pan Arab	2,653	1.18	78.6
Singapore	1,167	1.16	238.5
South Africa	2,029	1.21	38.3
South Korea	6,386	0.98	142.2
Spain	6,943	0.78	153.1
Sweden	2,024	0.65	220.5
Switzerland	2,724	0.83	372.4
Taiwan	1,886	0.59	92.0
Thailand	2,199	1.41	30.0
Turkey	1,372	0.46	12.4
UK	18,374	0.98	287.7
Uruguay	49	0.38	12.6
US	161,487	1.37	517.9
Venezuela	1,689	1.75	37.0
Vietnam	217	0.48	2.6
Total	365,036	0.99	74.8

Source: ZenithOptimedia

%	Newspapers	Magazines	TV	Radio	Cinema	Out-of-home	Internet
2003	30.3	13.8	37.0	9.0	0.4	5.4	3.2
2004	29.7	13.5	37.6	8.9	0.4	5.2	3.6
2005	29.5	13.4	37.7	8.7	0.4	5.2	3.9
2006	29.4	13.4	37.7	8.6	0.4	5.1	4.1
2007	29.2	13.4	37.6	8.6	0.4	5.1	4.4

Note: 2004 is estimate; 2005–07 are forecasts.
Source: ZenithOptimedia

Some advertising triumphs

Absolut

In America, Absolut vodka is priced around 50% higher than Smirnoff, thanks to its whimsical Swedish heritage and the lasting power of a 25-year-old advertising campaign. Created by TBWA Advertising in 1980, the campaign made the bottle a star. The first ad featured a photograph of the bottle in a circle of light against a black background. The headline, "Absolut Perfection", had wit and style and the idea led to more than 1,000 individual ads. Executions have evolved from the early classic formula – a photograph of the product and a punchy two-word headline – to include abstract interpretations of the bottle and its appeal. Many of the classic ads – such as 1983's "Absolut Attraction" in which a martini glass bends towards the bottle – still run. The longevity of the campaign is a rarity in the fickle world of advertising where accounts change hands faster than you can say "cheers".

Apple

Apple's "1984" commercial is viewed by many in the United States as the greatest TV ad of all time. In it Ridley Scott directed dramatic scenes of an Orwellian nightmare of tyranny and enslavement in which it was hinted that Big Brother and IBM were one and the same. The commercial featured ranks of automatons parted by an Amazonian heroine who hurled a hammer at an icon on the screen. "1984" has generated more than its fair share of myths and half-truths. The most often-made claim, that it ran only once, is incorrect. It aired during the 1984 Superbowl, in other regional centres and, cheekily, in Florida to target staff at IBM's PC unit HQ. The battle between individuality and doom actually acted as more of a tactical than a continuous campaign – with the agency asked to create an ad that would stop people buying IBM's new PC for a month until the Macintosh was on the shelves. Still, over 30 years later clients spend hundreds of millions of dollars on Superbowl spots in an effort to top "1984". To date, they are still trying.

Barclaycard

When credit cards first became popular in the UK in the 1970s what hampered their take-up was consumers' fear of over-spending. By the 1990s, the message that needed to be pushed was the usefulness of credit cards. Enter a hugely successful campaign starring Rowan Atkinson as the bungling secret agent Richard Latham. Although equipped with a Barclaycard in the ads, Latham was always dismissive about its usefulness. It was left to his assistant, Bough, to demonstrate the benefits of the card and get his boss out of numerous sticky situations. The campaign helped Barclaycard reverse a declining market share and achieve brand leadership.

Energizer

The DDB Needham agency in Chicago is the Energizer Bunny's birth mother, having created the first ad that featured the drum-pounding pink mascot gatecrashing a competition of other battery-operated toy rabbits in 1988. Later that year, TBWA in California became the adoptive agency that nurtured the bunny and it still has the business. The campaign was notable for the legal tussle between Energizer's owner Ralston Purina Co and Duracell's owner Gillette, which has also used a pink bunny mascot in its ads. It also became memorable for Energizer's

> **the unstoppable rabbit… hijacking commercials for everything from nasal sprays to soft drinks**

witty hijacking of ads for other products on TV. In these, a 60-second ad would be split into three 20-second segments, with the unstoppable rabbit apparently hijacking commercials for everything from nasal sprays to soft drinks. With staying power an intrinsic part of the initial idea, the longer this campaign runs the stronger the point about the product's attribute.

Gallaher

Tobacco advertising is now banned in the UK but in the 1980s, when Gallaher's agency Collett Dickenson Pearce launched the "Happiness is a cigar called Hamlet" campaign, the public was won over. Its consistently droll humour and use of Bach's "Air on a G String" helped the campaign become part of the nation's collective television-watching memory. Among the classics are

some advertising triumphs *continued*

"Photo booth", with a man struggling to get his straggly haired head in the frame in a passport photo booth. Another featured a man in a neck brace trying to follow the ball at a tennis match. Yet another (this one based on a news story about a Japanese golfer in a major tournament) featured a hapless golfer digging himself deeper into his bunker. Hamlet achieved a 40% market share of cigars before the TV advertising ban was introduced in 1991.

Levi Strauss

Bartle Bogle Hegarty's UK "launderette" commercial for Levi's was a benchmark commercial of the 1980s, simultaneously sexy and nostalgic. Beautifully directed, the ad was set in the territory of late 1950s America and a small-town launderette. To the astonishment of onlookers, a young man (model Nick Kamen) calmly strips and chucks his jeans in the machine together with a bagful of stones (viewers are told Levi's 501 jeans are now available stone-washed). Marvin Gaye's "I heard it through the grapevine" accompanied the ad and was re-released by Motown with the 501 logo on the sleeve – an example of integrated marketing almost before the term was invented. The ad was instrumental in reviving a sagging jeans market and a year after it aired, sales were up 800%. It was official: from the most cryptic of advertising briefs ("The right look. The right label") Levi's had been catapulted back to the frontline of popular culture.

> **a young man calmly strips and chucks his jeans in the machine**

Lynx/Axe

Unilever-owned Lever Fabergé, which owns Lynx (branded Axe outside the UK), engineered a turnaround in the brand's fortunes thanks to Bartle Bogle Hegarty. When first charged with reviving this marginal brand in Unilever's portfolio, BBH quickly realised that the macho commercials the brand was producing weren't fooling anyone. They engineered a 180-degree turn to put the brand's tongue firmly in its cheek via storylines where babes throw themselves all over unlikely male heroes. This is supposed to dramatise the Lynx Effect: that people are attracted to you when you smell of Lynx (not to be confused with smelling of lynx, which is liable to get you shot and stuffed). A recent commercial, which has run in Europe for two years, is for the Lynx deodorant range, which is claimed to work 24 hours a day. What happens? A young couple wake up in bed, then retrace their steps to where they met. They walk through a town and other public areas, picking up and getting dressed in various items of clothing they have removed on the way. In the final scene the couple return to their original meeting point – a supermarket aisle, with their two abandoned trolleys still sitting side by side. It ends with the line: "Because you never know when. Lynx 24-7 lasts 24 hours a day."

> **not to be confused with smelling of lynx, which would get you shot and stuffed**

Playtex

The most talked-about poster series of the 1990s was an aggressive pan-European campaign for the Playtex Wonderbra by agency TBWA. It took a product usually confined to the pages of women's magazines and ran it across giant billboards with provocative lines and arresting images. The most famous showed model Eva Herzigova glancing down at her Wonderbra-clad cleavage and the line "Hello Boys". Although the double entendre was unclear – was she talking to passers-by on the street, is there a gaggle of men on her doorstep or is she calling her breasts boys? – a relatively small adspend (just £300,000) garnered enormous publicity and Playtex's sales rose 41% year on year. The background to the campaign was a saga dubbed "Bra Wars" by the media: when the Sara Lee Corporation acquired the licence of Canadian lingerie maker Candelle and awarded it to its UK-owned Playtex, rival Courtaulds launched the Gossard Ultrabra. This business battle for products to enhance the fuller figure helped put bosoms firmly back on the fashion agenda.

Stella

Stella Artois, with around a 25% share of the market, is the UK's top-selling premium lager on the back of a continuing series of commercials by the Lowe agency which began in 1992. This expensive campaign – which has been extended to Australia, New Zealand and parts of eastern Europe, uses the "Reassuringly

some advertising triumphs *continued*

expensive" slogan and focuses on the things you might be prepared to sacrifice for a glass of Stella. Really, they shouldn't work, for the dialogue is usually in French, the stories they tell are long-winded and the humour tortuous. Yet Stella's UK sales are higher than the entire Whitbread-owned brand's other world markets combined. The latest commercial in the series was shot in black and white over ten days in the Czech Republic. Complete with a dogfight scene starring replica first world war planes, the two-minute commercial tells the story of an English Sopwith Camel pilot shot down over occupied France and his bid for freedom. Having limped to the sanctuary of a village, he is hidden by the barman. Ordered to remain still by a passing German patrol, the barman only reveals the pilot's hiding place when a pouring Stella Artois beer tap looks set to overflow.

Volkswagen

After the conspicuous consumption of the1980s, no campaign expressed the essence of the more sober pre-dotcom 1990s better than Volkswagen's by BMP DDB (now just DDB). Simple but devastatingly effective, one commercial showed workmen cladding a lamp-post to cushion passers-by who walked into it distracted by a poster advertising the VW Polo L's low price (only £8,265). In a world in which too many car commercials feature the same advertising clichés – winding roads, gleaming metal, thumping music – consumers responded to the style of this confident and pared-down campaign. Another ad in the series,

❝workmen cladding a lamp-post to cushion passers-by who walked into it❞

this time a press execution, showed an out-of-focus bride and groom, the photographer having zoomed instead onto a passing bus-side, advertising the Polo for just £8,290.

Three advertising bloomers

British Rail – "We're getting there"

Step forward the British Rail campaign of 1984, based on the line "We're getting there". Honest? Perhaps, but admitting to even the tiniest fault is not a practice an advertiser usually engages in even when its own research and that of 14 agencies convince it that honesty is the best policy. The company had spent £35m over the previous five years trying to convince commuters that the 1980s were "the age of the train". So when BR opted for the "We're getting there" line the media had a field day suggesting that BR may have thought it was getting there but its overcrowded trains most certainly were not.

Mr Kipling – nativity play

The original Mr Kipling ads featured "Mr Kipling" making a hash of various tasks he undertakes but he is forgiven because he makes "exceedingly good" cakes. An exceedingly large row was created by an ad for Mr Kipling that opened with a woman called Mary giving birth. As the camera pulled back, it emerged that she was on stage in front of a horrified audience at a nativity

the ad opened with a woman called Mary giving birth…on stage

play. A stunned woman asked a vicar (who is eating a Mr Kipling mince pie) if the cakemaker has ever directed before. "No", came the answer, "but he does make…" etc. The commercial, the most complained-about ad of 2004, was taken off air after it provoked an unholy 797 calls to Ofcom, the TV regulator, from people who said it made a mockery of a religious event, could upset children and was demeaning to women because it trivialised the act of giving birth.

Burger King – Herb

Beginning in late 1985, Burger King ran a campaign in the United States centred on a balding nerd named Herb. The unfathomably stupid premise was that Herb was a loser so clueless he hadn't sampled Burger King's grilled-rather-than-fried excellence. He did nothing for burger sales and indeed was such a humiliation for everyone involved that the agency which devised the campaign soon lost the business in what was at the time the biggest account change in advertising history.

Some famous advertising slogans " "

"All the news that's fit to print." *New York Times* (1896)

"I'd walk a mile for a Camel." Camel (1921)

"Ask the man who owns one." Packard (1925)

"Guinness is good for you." Guinness (1929)

"Snap! Crackle! Pop!" Kellogg's Rice Krispies (1932)

"Don't be vague. Ask for Haig." Haig Scotch Whisky (1934)

"If you want to get ahead, get a hat." Hat Council (1934)

"A diamond is forever." De Beers (1948)

"A little dab'll do ya." Brylcreem (1949)

"Finger lickin' good." Kentucky Fried Chicken (1952)

"The milk chocolate melts in your mouth, not in your hand."
    M&Ms (1954)

"You'll wonder where the yellow went when you brush your teeth
    with Pepsodent." Pepsodent (1956)

"Go to work on an egg." UK Egg Marketing Board (1957)

"Think small." Volkswagen (1962)

"We try harder." Avis (1962)

"Schhh … You-Know-Who." Schweppes (1962)

"Put a tiger in your tank" Esso (1964)

"A Mars a day helps you work, rest and play." Mars (1965)

"Beanz Meanz Heinz." Heinz (1967)

"Say it with flowers" Interflora (1971)

"Probably the best beer in the world." Carlsberg (1973)

"Lipsmackin' thirstquenchin' acetastin' motivatin' goodbuzzin'
    cooltalkin' highwalkin' fastlivin' evergivin' coolfizzin' Pepsi."
    Pepsi Cola (1973)

"Heineken refreshes the parts other beers cannot reach." Heineken
    (1974)

"Don't leave home without it." American Express (1975)

"The ultimate driving machine." BMW (1975)

"The world's favourite airline" British Airways (1983)

"Vorsprung durch technik." Audi (1984)

"When it absolutely, positively, has to be there
    overnight." Federal Express (1982)

"Just do it." Nike (1988)

"Think different." Apple Macintosh (1998)

Some business giants of the past

Carnegie, Andrew (1835–1919)

The richest man ever to come out of Dumfermline, Andrew Carnegie left Scotland for Pittsburgh, Pennsylvania, with his family in search of work after the introduction of the mechanical loom put his weaver father out of work. Carnegie's first job was as a bobbin boy in a textile factory. After later jobs as a clerk and a messenger boy, in 1853 he became assistant to Tom Scott, the superintendent of the Pennsylvania Railroad's western division. He started investing on his own behalf in iron manufacturing and other businesses, and made substantial returns. In 1859 he was promoted to the position of superintendent and in 1865 he resigned from the railroad to concentrate on business, in particular iron and steel. The civil war had fuelled demand for iron, as had the move to replace wooden bridges with iron ones and, most important of all, the expansion of the railroads. Carnegie introduced the Bessemer steel process to America, which meant that steel could be produced at greater speed and lower cost, with the result that the Carnegie Steel Company was producing a quarter of America's steel by 1900 and was making a profit of $40m. Carnegie believed that great wealth was of no value unless it was put to good use and he wrote several treatises on this theme, including the *Gospel of Wealth* in which he argued that any riches beyond those needed for the survival of one's family should be used for the good of the wider community. By the time he sold his company to J. P. Morgan in 1901 for $480m, Carnegie had already spent a great deal of money in accordance with his principles. As a self-educated but cultivated man, he was a great believer in public libraries and he spent over $50m setting up some 2,500 of them. By the time he died, he had given away $350m.

> **Carnegie believed that great wealth was of no value unless it was put to good use**

Disney, Walt Elias (1901–66)

Walt Disney was a sentimentalist whose somewhat rigid idea of America on occasions gave his work a sinister edge. The inventor and voice of Mickey Mouse also produced cheery military

some business **giants** of the past *continued*

propaganda like *Victory Through Airpower* and in 1947 appeared before the House Committee on Un-American Activities to name employees he said were communist infiltrators: "I really feel that they ought to be smoked out for what they are so that all the liberalisms that really are American can go out without the taint of communism". Between 1942 and 1943, 95% of Disney Studios' output was on contract to the US government and Disney was particularly proud of his contribution to the tax-take after *The New Spirit* explained the importance of declaring your income for tax.

He was born in Chicago, left school to drive an ambulance for the Red Cross in France aged 16 and returned from there, having survived influenza in the great epidemic, in 1919. Walt began drawing cartoons and set up a little company, Laugh-O-Gram Films, before moving to Hollywood. There he brought Oswald the Lucky Rabbit into existence and then Mickey Mouse, who appeared with synchronised sound. Walt Disney was among the first to recognise the importance of sound for bringing cartoons, and later nature films, to life. He also pioneered Technicolor, winning an Academy Award for *Flowers and Trees* in 1932. The combination of these successes led to a feature-length cartoon

> **❝ Walt was among the first to recognise the importance of sound ❞**

and *Snow White and the Seven Dwarves* opened in 1937. The profits ran to millions and Disney set about constructing $3m offices that would churn out the now familiar Disney cartoons.

He returned to bulk-making cartoons after the war, but also continued with informational films such as those about NASA which he made with the help of ex-Nazi Wernher von Braun, inventor of the V2 Rocket. Disneyland opened in 1955 in Anaheim, California, and there were other theme-parks on the horizon. These perhaps helped formulate an idea in Walt's mind that he called EPCOT (Experimental Prototype Community of Tomorrow). But he died before he was able to see its fruition.

Ford, Henry (1863–1947)

Henry Ford is best known for the invention of the Model T Ford and the moving assembly line and less well-known as the US publisher of the notorious anti-semitic *Protocols of the Elders of Zion* (in his newspaper *The Dearborn Independent*). Ford was born to Irish immigrant parents from County Cork and left the family farm to work as a machinist in Detroit. He returned to work on the family farm in 1882 but was shortly afterwards taken on, thanks to his skills with steam engines, as a maintenance engineer in a local company. In 1891 he joined the Edison Illuminating Company but found sufficient spare time to invent, build and drive his Quadricycle which led to the creation of the Henry Ford Company. This, however, was taken over by the investors who turned it into Cadillac, so Henry Ford set up the Ford motor company in 1903 and released the Model T six years later. In 1918, half of all cars in America were Model T Fords. Ford's approach to his workers was paternalistic but combined the generous treatment of suitable workers with suppression of union activity.

Gibbs, William (1790–1875)

"Mr Gibbs made his tibbs selling turds of foreign birds." One of the sons of Anthony Gibbs, William built churches and the grand house of Tyntesfield near Bristol with money made from guano. Guano is seabird dung, rich in nitrates and phosphates, and was harvested in earnest off South America's coast from the middle of the 19th century as fertiliser. William and his brother George signed their first contract with the Peruvian government in 1842 and in 1858 imported 300,000 tons of guano to Britain. William was able to build Tyntesfield at a cost of £70,000, the profits of just one year's trade. (In 2002 the house was acquired by the National Trust for £25m.) He also paid for churches to be built elsewhere, including the chapel of Keble College, Oxford.

Ray Kroc (1902–84)

It was Ray Kroc who persuaded Dick and Mac McDonald to expand and set up their restaurants across the United States, and to employ him to oversee this project. At the age of 15, Ray Kroc, who had lied about his age, had been destined for Europe as a Red Cross ambulance driver. He was saved by the war ending before he could leave and began instead a variety of salesman's jobs. He first met the McDonald brothers when selling mixing machines for restaurants; their purchase of eight of these machines gave him the idea for setting up identikit restaurants like theirs. Kroc prided

some business **giants** of the past *continued*

himself on his standards of quality, service and cleanliness, and he
believed that there should be no reservations, no waiting and low
prices. There was no doubt, however, about
his core principle – in his own words: "The
definition of salesmanship is the gentle art of
letting the customer have it your way." He
was chairman of the McDonald's
Corporation from its creation in 1955 until

> **salesmanship is the gentle art of letting the customer have it *your* way**

his death and he never stopped developing new ideas, from
German taverns to theme parks. When his widow, Joan, died in
2004, she left a bequest of £800m to the Salvation Army.

Krupp, Alfred (1812–87)

Alfred Krupp was an outstanding businessman and engineer who
profited from industrialisation and war in Europe. Born in Essen
into a family of metal-workers, he began work in the family iron
forge when his father fell ill. Together with his mother, who took
control of the firm on the death of her husband in 1826, Alfred
began building on the possibilities presented by the manufacture
of steel. The firm became a central element in the building of the
railways and produced, among other railway components, the
seamless wheel tyre. Increasingly, however, Alfred was looking to
armaments for the company's survival – he had produced its first
steel gun in 1847. In 1848, he became the head of the company
and began in earnest the acquisition of mines, docks and
collieries in order to guarantee the raw materials that he needed.
By the time of his death, Krupps employed 20,200 people and
had instituted a rule that the company could only be passed to a
single heir. Later, the Krupps firm would produce the artillery
used to shell Paris in first world war ("Big Bertha"). The Krupp
whose collaboration with Adolf Hitler led to the break-up of the
Krupp empire was in fact Gustav von Bohlen und Halbach, who
changed his name when he married Alfred's granddaughter
Bertha.

William Hesketh Lever (1851–1925)

Born in Bolton in the north of England, Lever was a pioneering
manufacturer of soap who applied his wealth to a variety of good

causes. In 1886, he was the founding partner in Lever Brothers with James Lever. In the course of their business, they made the discovery that soap could be made from vegetable oil instead of tallow and from that discovery came Sunlight soap – hence Port Sunlight, the model village near Liverpool that Lever built for his workers. After his purchase of the Scottish islands of Harris and Lewis in 1918, he established similar projects there, too, and spent large sums of money trying to create a gainfully employed community free from poverty. Lever is known for his art collections, which served a dual purpose, for not only did he have a passion for art and artefacts, but he also saw that certain types of painting could be used to promote soap sales. These tended to be illustrations of pristine clothes worn by happy but poor people. The artists were not always happy to find their creations used in this way. However, after his wife's death in 1913, Lever built a gallery in her memory where the pictures and other collections are preserved. Lever's pre-eminence in business and social zeal were recognised by a series of titles. He was MP for the Wirral and was made a baronet. He was raised to the peerage as Lord Leverhulme of Bolton-le-Moors in 1917 and became Viscount Leverhulme of the Isles five years later. To this day, money left by him is given to research and education projects.

> he saw that certain types of painting could be used to promote soap sales

Morgan, John Pierpoint (1837–1913)

The richest man in America by 1900, John Pierpoint Morgan made his money through the financing of debt and the control of important US industries. He rescued America's finances on more than one occasion, notably helping to refinance the civil war debt and bailing out Wall Street during its financial crisis in 1907. Born into a banking family, Morgan travelled widely when he was young and graduated from the University of Göttingen. After a stretch working as an accountant for the Duncan Sherman & Co banking house, he began working in as an accountant for a finance house that served George Peabody, his father's partner, in New York. His father, Junius Spencer, subsequently succeeded Peabody and renamed the company J. S. Morgan, which John Pierpoint joined in 1864. In 1895, he took over the bank, and it became J. P. Morgan. He began systematising the railroads and

some business **giants** of the past *continued*

gained stock in the railroad companies he reorganised; by 1900 he controlled 5,000 miles of railroad rights, one-sixth of the total. There followed the purchase and consolidation of US steel manufacturing – he bought the Carnegie Steel Company from Andrew Carnegie for $480m and joined it to his own Federal Steel Company in 1901. The resulting US Steel Corporation was the first company in the world to be capitalised at over $1 billion. In the meantime, he had also started the International Harvester Company, which dealt in agricultural equipment, and the International Mercantile Marine shipping company (owner of White Star Line, which built the Titanic). It was with reason that antitrust campaigners attacked him given that he controlled several industries almost in their entirety. In spite of the cathedral and churches he built, and his intervention to save Wall Street in 1907 (which eventually led to the creation of the Federal Reserve System), J. P. Morgan's reputation still hangs, somewhere between "robber baron" and builder of America's economy.

> **he rescued America finances on more than one occasion**

Morita, Akio (1921–99)

The man who conceived the idea of the Walkman was born into a Nagoya family that traded in sake and soy sauce. Instead of working in the family firm and ignoring his father's advice that he study economics, Morita chose to study electronics at Tokyo University. It was in his subsequent work in missile design that he met Masaru Ibuka with whom, in 1946, he set up Tokyo Telecommunications and Engineering Industries (Tokyo Tsushin Kogyo). Masaru was the source of much of the company's electrical engineering success but Morita provided the business sense that underlay the greatest achievements. He wanted to destroy the image of Japan as a source of cheap and shoddy goods and started selling the company's products abroad. In 1958 he rebranded the company as Sony (a combination of *sonus* (Latin: sound) and Sonny Boy), and in 1961 Sony was the first foreign company to be listed on the New York Stock Exchange. Morita retired from Sony in 1994. Henry Kissinger said that he was probably the most effective spokesman for Japan he ever met.

Rockefeller, John Davison (1839–1937)

The wealth of the Rockefellers was created by John Davison Rockefeller through control of oil production in the United States. He began as a book-keeper in a company buying and selling futures and then moved to an oil refinery in Ohio. In 1870, with several others, Rockefeller founded Standard Oil. The company grew in power through the acquisition of competing refineries and through control of the railroads. The scale of consolidation was such that Standard Oil came under attack from the antitrust movement and in 1911 was ordered by the US Supreme Court to be broken up; many new small companies were formed from its ruins. But the Rockefeller fortune had been made. John Rockefeller was reckoned to be worth $900m in 1901 and, one of the modern age's great philanthropists, had given away $500m by the time he died; he had founded the University of Chicago, the Rockefeller Institute for Medical Research and The Rockefeller Foundation to "promote the well-being of mankind" and had supported many other organisations and institutions. It was his son, John Davison Rockefeller II, who built the Rockefeller Centre in New York.

> one of the great philanthopists, he had given away **$500 million** by the time he died

Woolworth, Frank (1852–1919)

Frank Woolworth originally conceived the idea of selling goods at discounted and fixed prices when he observed the attraction discount stalls of leftovers held for customers. He reasoned that this was because of the price but also because people liked seeing and handling the goods. On this basis he set up the first of his stores in 1879. His misjudgment on this occasion was to sell goods at only five cents and the shop went bust. Undeterred, he proceeded to set up new stores which offered goods at both five and ten cents (hence "five and ten cents stores"). After one or two further failures the business started to grow, and by 1904 there were 120 Woolworths stores in 21 states across America. On his death in 1919, Woolworth had established more than 1,000 stores in America and elsewhere and a $65m corporation had been formed. Woolworth built the eponymous tower in New York which was the tallest in the world at the time.

Philanthr ♥ py and the non-profit sector

America's most generous philanthropists

	Background	2000–04 given or pledged, $bn
Bill & Melinda Gates	Microsoft co-founder	10.09
Gordon & Betty Moore	Intel co-founder	7.05
Warren Buffett	Berkshire Hathaway CEO	2.72
George Soros	Investor	2.30
James & Virginia Stowers	American Century founder	1.25
Eli & Edythe Broad	SunAmerica, KB Home founder	1.33
Michael & Susan Dell	Dell founder	0.93
Alfred Mann	Medical devices	0.83
Paul Allen	Microsoft co-founder	0.74
Walton Family	Family of Wal-Mart founder	0.65
Ruth Lilly	Eli Lilly heiress	0.56
Veronica Atkins	Widow of Dr Atkins	0.50

Source: *BusinessWeek*

Britain's most generous philanthropists

	Background	2002 given, £m
Sainsbury family	Supermarkets	45.30
Weston family	Bread and tea	39.90
Lord Rothschild	Banking	33.80
Leverhulme family	Founders of Unilever	23.00
Laing family	Construction	8.80
Fleming family	Banking	8.60
Sir Leslie & Dame Shirley Porter	Tesco supermarkets	5.40
Cadbury family	Confectionery, food and drink	5.20
Weinstock family	Industrialists	4.72
Peter Ogden	Co-founder of Computacenter	4.42

Sources: CaritasData; *The Sunday Times*

Causes	Estimated lifetime giving, $bn	Donations as % of net worth
Health, education, information access	27.98	58
Environmental conservation, science	7.30	192
Reproductive choice, reducing nuclear weapons	2.73	8
Open and free societies	5.17	72
Biomedical research	1.56	218
Public education, arts, science	1.57	26
Children's health & education	1.23	9
Biomedical education & research	1.00	71
Arts, culture	0.83	4
Education	1.00	1
Poetry, libraries, culture	0.75	250
Eradication of diabetes	0.50	100

The health of the non-profit sector

2004	Capacity	Sustainability	Impact	Overall
Netherlands	79	54	89	74
Norway	55	82	59	65
US	76	54	54	61
Sweden	58	56	67	60
UK	66	60	50	58
Belgium	65	45	60	57
Ireland	64	45	52	54
Australia	51	46	49	49
France	56	46	44	49
Finland	48	42	50	47
Germany	47	45	47	46
Spain	54	37	30	40
Average	45	39	36	40

Note: Scores out of 100 on the Johns Hopkins Global Civil Society Index (GCSI), which measures the level of development of the civil society sector in 34 countries. Capacity refers to the level of effort the sector mobilises; sustainability refers to the ability of civil society to survive over time; impact refers to the contribution that civil society makes to social, economic and political life.
Source: Johns Hopkins University

The richest people

World, 1996

	Worth, $bn	Country/region
Bill Gates	18.5	US
Warren Buffett	15.0	US
Paul Sacher, Oeri & Hoffman, family	13.1	Switzerland
Lee Shau Kee	12.7	Hong Kong
Tsai Wan-lin, family	12.2	Taiwan
Kwok, brothers	11.2	Hong Kong
Li Ka-shing, family	10.6	Hong Kong
Yoshiaki Tsutsumi	9.2	Japan
Theo & Karl Albrecht	9.0	Germany
Hans & Gad Rausing	9.0	Scandinavia
Johanna, Susanne & Stefan Quandt	8.1	Germany
Haniel, family	8.1	Germany
Paul Allen	7.5	US
Kenneth Thomson	7.4	Canada
John Werner Kluge	7.2	US

World, 2004

	Worth, $bn	Country/region
Bill Gates	46.6	US
Warren Buffett	42.9	US
Karl Albrecht	23.0	Germany
Prince Alwaleed Bin Talal Alsaud	21.5	Saudi Arabia
Paul Allen	21.0	US
Alice Walton	20.0	US
Helen Walton	20.0	US
Jim Walton	20.0	US
John Walton	20.0	US
Robson Walton	20.0	US
Liliane Bettencourt	18.8	France
Lawrence Ellison	18.7	US
Ingvar Kamprad	18.5	Sweden
Theo Albrecht	18.1	Germany
Kenneth Thomson & family	17.2	Canada

Source: *Forbes*

Britain, 2005

	Worth, $bn	Country/region
Lakshmi Mittal	14.80	Steel
Roman Abramovich	7.50	Oil, industry and football
Duke of Westminster	5.60	Property
Hans Rausing & family	4.95	Food packaging
Philip & Christina Green	4.85	Retail
Oleg Deripaska	4.38	Aluminium
Sir Richard Branson	3.00	Transport and mobile phones
Kirsten & Jorn Rausing	2.58	Inheritance and investments
David & Simon Reuben	2.50	Property and metal trading
Spiro Latsis & family	2.40	Banking, aviation and shipping
Bernie & Slavica Ecclestone	2.32	Motor racing
Charlene & Michel de Carvalho	2.27	Inheritance, brewing and banking
Mahdi al-Tajir	2.10	Oil, investments and bottled water
Sri & Gopi Hinduja	2.10	Industry and finance
Joe Lewis	2.00	Foreign exchange dealing

Source: *Sunday Times* Rich List, 2005

Russia, 2004

	Worth, $bn	Country/region
Mikhail Khodorkovsky	15.2	Yukos
Roman Abramovich	12.5	Sibneft, Russian Aluminium
Viktor Vekselberg	5.9	TNK-BP, SUAL-Holding
Mikhail Prokhorov	5.4	Norilsk Nickel
Vladimir Potanin	5.4	Norilsk Nickel
Mikhail Fridman	5.2	Alfa-Group
Vladimir Lisin	4.8	Novolipetsk Metallurgical
Oleg Deripaska	4.5	Russian Aluminium
Alexei Mordashov	4.5	Severstal Group
Vagit Alekperov	3.9	Lukoil
Gherman Khan	2.9	Alfa-Group
Alexander Abramov	2.4	Evraz Holding
Vladimir Bogdanov	2.2	Surgutneftegaz
Vladimir Yevtushenkov	2.1	AFK Sistema, Mobile Telesystems
Iskander Makhmudov	2.1	UGMK

Source: *Forbes*

Central bankers since 1900

Bank of England governors

	Year appointed
Samuel Steuart Gladstone	1899
Sir Augustus Prevost	1901
Samuel Hope Morley	1903
Alexander Falconer Wallace	1905
William Middleton Campbell	1907
Reginald Eden Johnston	1909
Alfred Clayton Cole	1911
Walter Cunliffe	1913
Sir Brien Ibrican Cokayne	1918
Montagu Collet Norman	1920
Lord Catto of Cairncatto	1944
Cameron Fromanteel Cobbold	1949
The Earl of Cromer	1961
Leslie Kenneth O'Brien	1966
Gordon William Humphreys Richardson	1973
Robert (Robin) Leigh-Pemberton	1983
Edward Alan John George	1993
Mervyn Allister King	2003

US Federal Reserve chairmen

	Year appointed
Charles S. Hamlin	1914
W. P. G. Harding	1916
Daniel R Crissinger	1923
Roy A. Young	1927
Eugene Meyer	1930
Eugene R. Black	1933
Marriner S. Eccles	1934
Thomas B. McCabe	1948
Wm McC Martin, Jr	1951
Arthur F. Burns	1970
G. William Miller	1978
Paul A. Volcker	1979
Alan Greenspan	1987

European Central Bank presidents

	Year appointed
Willem F. Duisenberg	1998
Jean-Claude Trichet	2003

Bank of Japan presidents

	Year appointed
Tatsuo Yamamoto	1898
Baron Shigeyoshi Matsuo	1903
Korekiyo Takahashi	1911
Viscount Yataro Mishima	1913
Junnosuke Inoue	1919
Otohiko Ichiki	1923
Junnosuke Inoue	1927
Hisaakira Hijikata	1928
Eigo Fukai	1935
Seihin Ikeda	1937
Toyotaro Yuki	1937
Viscount Keizo Shibusawa	1944
Eikichi Araki	1945
Hisato Ichimada	1946
Eikichi Araki	1954
Masamichi Yamagiwa	1956
Makoto Usami	1964
Tadashi Sasaki	1969
Teiichiro Morinaga	1974
Haruo Mayekawa	1979
Satoshi Sumita	1984
Yasushi Mieno	1989
Yasuo Matsushita	1994
Masaru Hayami	1998
Toshihiko Fukui	2003

Sources: Central banks

"In their own words"

▪ Business is really more agreeable than pleasure; it interests the whole mind ... more deeply. But it does not look as if it did.
Walter Bagehot English journalist and author and early editor of *The Economist*

▪ We don't have a monopoly. We have market share. There's a difference.
Steve Ballmer CEO of Microsoft

▪ Every young man would do well to remember that all successful business stands on the foundation of morality.
Henry Ward Beecher 19th century American theologian

▪ Failing organisations are usually over-managed and under-led.
Warren G. Bennis management theorist

▪ If you can run one business well, you can run any business well.
Sir Richard Branson founder of Virgin group

▪ The market, like the Lord, helps those who help themselves. But unlike the Lord, the market does not forgive those who know not what they do.
Warren Buffett American investor

❝...but it does ▪ pay to be in a *hurry*❞

▪ In the search for companies to acquire we adopt the same attitude one might find appropriate in looking for a spouse: it pays to be active, interested and open minded, but it does not pay to be in a hurry.
Warren Buffet

▪ Some regard private enterprise as if it were a predatory tiger to be shot. Others look upon it as a cow that they can milk. Only a handful see it for what it really is – the strong horse that pulls the whole cart.
Winston Churchill British statesman

▪ The chief business of the American people is business.
Calvin Coolidge former American president

▪ Wherever you see a successful business, someone once made a courageous decision.
Peter Drucker American management theorist

- Most of what we call management consists of making it difficult for people to get their work done.

Peter Drucker

- Once I began following my own instincts, sales took off and I became a millionaire. And that, I think, is a key secret to every person's success, be they male or female, banker or pornographer: trust in your gut.

Larry Flynt pioneering American pornographer

- A business that makes nothing but money is a poor business.

Henry Ford American carmaker

- Your most unhappy customers are your greatest source of learning.

Bill Gates founder of Microsoft

- In the end, all business operations can be reduced to three words: people, product, and profits.

Lee Iacocca former CEO of Chrysler

- Sometimes when you innovate, you make mistakes. It is best to admit them quickly, and get on with improving your other innovations.

Steve Jobs founder of Apple Computer

- Markets can remain irrational longer than you can remain solvent.

John Maynard Keynes economist

- Business, more than any other occupation, is a continual dealing with the future; it is a continual calculation, an instinctive exercise in foresight.

Henry Luce American publisher

- Business is a combination of war and sport.

Andre Maurois French author

- The buck stops with the guy who signs the cheques.

Rupert Murdoch Australian-born media magnate

"in their own words" *continued*

■ The secret of business is to know something that nobody else knows.

Aristotle Onassis Greek shipping tycoon

■ Almost all quality improvement comes via simplification of design, manufacturing, layout, processes, and procedures.

Tom Peters management guru

■ A friendship founded on business is a good deal better than a business founded on friendship.

John D. Rockefeller American oilman

■ If you don't do it excellently, don't do it at all. Because if it's not excellent, it won't be profitable or fun, and if you're not in business for fun or profit, what the hell are you doing there?

Robert Townsend American businessman

■ My son is now an "entrepreneur." That's what you're called when you don't have a job.

Ted Turner founder of CNN

■ There is only one boss. The customer. And he can fire everybody in the company from the chairman on down, simply by spending his money somewhere else.

Sam Walton founder of Wal-Mart

> ❝❝there is only one boss: the customer❞

■ An organization's ability to learn, and translate that learning into action rapidly, is the ultimate competitive advantage.

Jack Welch former CEO of GE

■ In modern business it is not the crook who is to be feared most, it is the honest man who doesn't know what he is doing.

William Wordsworth English poet

Bad boys – and one bad girl

Ivan Boesky, an American arbitrageur, coined the phrase "greed is good" that symbolised the ethos of many of those working in the financial markets during the 1980s. Mr Boesky made his cash betting on corporate takeovers but he did not rely on luck and judgment alone. He was convicted of insider dealing, a crime often overlooked in those freewheeling days on Wall Street, yet the blatancy of his actions earned him three-and-a-half years in prison and a fine of $100m even after plea bargaining and informing on many of his sources.

Bernie Cornfeld, a social worker turned mutual-fund salesman, decided to start his own operation in the 1960s. Investors Overseas Services (IOS) was based in Geneva to escape regulation and targeted ex-pat Americans seeking to avoid income tax, although some half his investors were German, also lured by his pitch – "Do you seriously want to be rich?". After ten years, IOS had raised

> **do you seriously want to be rich?**

$2.5 billion and had 1m shareholders. IOS, in effect a glorified Ponzi scheme (see Charles Ponzi below), collapsed in 1970. Cornfeld spent 11 months in a Swiss jail before fraud charges were finally dropped.

Bernie Ebbers, a cowboy-hat and boot wearing businessman and former night-club bouncer, built WorldCom from modest beginnings into a telecoms firm worth over $175 billion at the height of the stockmarket boom by relentlessly acquiring assets. In 1998, he masterminded a $37 billion merger with MCI, one of America's leading long-distance phone companies. But as the dotcom boom ran out of steam, WorldCom resorted to accounting tricks to maintain the appearance of ever-growing profitability. The fraud failed to keep the company afloat. In April 2002, Mr Ebbers was forced to step down as chief executive and later the firm admitted an $11 billion accounting fraud, resulting in America's biggest-ever bankruptcy. In 2004, Mr Ebbers was found guilty of fraud, conspiracy and filing false documents with regulators, and was sentenced in July 2005 to 25 years in jail.

Martin Frankel, an American money manager, was arrested in Germany in 1999 after an international manhunt. He was reportedly in possession of nine fake passports, 547 diamonds, an astrological chart drawn up to answer the question "Will I go to prison?" and a to-do list that included "launder money". In 2002, Mr Frankel pleaded guilty to 24 federal corruption charges for defrauding more than $200m from insurance companies in the southern United States. His technique was to buy small insurance firms and help himself to their assets in order to fund his lavish lifestyle. He was sentenced to 17 years in prison in 2004.

Ivar Kreuger, "the Swedish match king", gained monopolies for match production in many countries after the first world war. He then set up the International Match Corporation in America, which went on to control two-thirds of world match production. But his business began to fail after the Wall Street crash of 1929 and he hit a liquidity crisis. He was found dead in a hotel room in Paris in 1932 having seemingly shot himself. After his death, it was discovered that, through false accounting, American investors had been fleeced of millions of dollars.

Nick Leeson worked for Barings, a respectable and long-established bank based in the City of London. His work, trading futures on the Singapore Monetary Exchange, led to big losses when bets on the future direction of the Japanese stockmarket went spectacularly wrong after the Kobe earthquake of 1995 sent Asian markets plummeting. He kept the losses hidden from his superiors and made a series of increasingly risky investments in an effort to recoup the cash. These failed, and when his losses hit $1.4 billion Mr Leeson went on the run. He was apprehended in Germany and sent back to Singapore where he was sentenced to six-and-a-half years in prison. Barings collapsed and was bought by ING, a Dutch insurance giant, for the nominal sum of £1.

Michael Milken, the "junk bond king" of Wall Street, financed a slew of corporate takeovers in the 1980s through the pioneering use of high-yield high-risk bonds, making vast sums for himself and his employer, Drexel Burnham Lambert, in the process. He and co-conspirators constructed a web of deceitful transactions that led to 98 charges of racketeering, insider trading and securities fraud, and in 1989, he was sentenced to ten years in prison for securities fraud – "the greatest criminal conspiracy the financial world has ever known". In 1991 his sentence was reduced to two years in prison and three years' probation. In 1998 he settled with the government, paying $42m plus interest. Since then Mr Milken has devoted much of his time and money to charity work.

Robert Maxwell was born Jan Ludwik Hoch in Czechoslovakia in 1923. He fled the Nazis in 1939 and fought with the British during the second world war, calling himself du Maurier, after a brand of classy cigarettes. After the war he came to Britain and changed his name to Maxwell. In 1951 he purchased Pergamon Press, publisher of textbooks and scientific journals, and published a lot of material from communist eastern Europe, where he developed good connections. In 1964 he became a Labour member of parliament, but a financial scandal put an end to his political career five years later. However, in 1974 the "bouncing Czech" repurchased Pergamon, over which he had lost control, and during the 1980s he built up a substantial publishing empire, which included Macmillan, a big US publisher, and Britain's Mirror Group Newspapers. As the 1980s progressed Maxwell's financial machinations began to catch up with him. In 1991 it was reported that Maxwell had disappeared from his luxury motor yacht off the Canary Islands and not long after his body was found floating some distance away. After he was buried on the Mount of Olives overlooking Jerusalem, it emerged that he had looted £400m from the Mirror Group's pension fund to prop up his other business interests. Did he jump or was he pushed? Some claim that Mossad agents were behind his death. It is more likely, however, that he knew the game was finally up and couldn't face the consequences.

> **it emerged that he had looted £400m from the Mirror Group's pension fund**

Asil Nadir, the former boss of Polly Peck International, a British-based conglomerate that included an electronics business and the Del Monte fruit business acquired through a series of audacious acquisitions, fled to northern Cyprus to take advantage of its lack of an extradition treaty with Britain (which does not recognise the territory) after the firm collapsed with previously concealed debts of over £1 billion. The businessman, who had made generous donations to Britain's Conservative Party (to its subsequent embarrassment), was facing 66 charges of theft amounting to

£34m but fled by private jet in 1993, shortly before he was due to stand trial. He still lives in northern Cyprus with the hope that one day he will be able to cut a deal that will allow him to return to Britain.

Charles Ponzi was born in Italy and moved to America in 1903, taking a series of menial jobs before launching a scheme in 1919 that promised to double investors' money in 90 days. By 1920 he had taken millions of dollars by paying former investors with later deposits, thus requiring ever greater numbers of dupes to join the scam. The business collapsed only after 40,000 people had handed over some $15m. Despite a wrangle over jurisdiction, Ponzi got five years in federal prison for mail fraud and was later sentenced to seven to nine years in Massachusetts. He jumped bail and started up a new scheme in Florida based on selling land. This collapsed and he received another year in jail, and was sent back to Boston to serve his former sentence. Ponzi died in poverty in Rio de Janeiro in 1949 but his legacy is the pyramid-selling schemes that still bear his name.

Frank Quattrone, a star investment banker in the dotcom boom, was found guilty of obstructing justice in 2004. He instructed his staff to "clean up" files before an investigation by regulators into "spinning", the practice of allocating tranches of new shares in hot technology firms to favoured clients in return for lucrative investment-banking business. He was sentenced to 18 months behind bars but was set free pending an appeal.

Martha Stewart, a hugely wealthy American lifestyle and homemaking guru, was found guilty in 2004 of trying to make a little extra on the side. She was accused of obstructing justice and lying to investigators probing the sale of shares in a drug company days before the release of bad news about one of its products sent its shares plummeting. She was sentenced to five months in prison and home detention for the same period, and fined $30,000.

Yoshiaki Tsutsumi was briefly adjudged the world's richest man at the height of Japan's property boom in the late 1980s, having inherited a real estate business from his father who was once said to have owned a sixth of all the land in Japan. But in 2005 Mr Tsutsumi, one of Japan's best-known businessmen, was arrested on suspicion of falsifying shareholder information and selling shares based on the false data. He pleaded guilty and faced up to eight years in jail.

Robert Vesco got involved with Bernie Cornfeld's IOS (see above) as a "white knight" to save the foundering fund. He was later accused of looting the company of $224m and fled to Costa Rica after making large illegal contributions to Richard Nixon's re-election campaign. He was charged *in absentia* with theft (and drug smuggling, for good measure). In 1996, Mr Vesco was sentenced to 13 years in prison in Cuba on charges of producing and marketing a miracle cancer cure to overseas investors without the communist government's knowledge.

... and – but for Andrew Fastow – the jury is still out on

Enron became one of the world's largest energy firms by trading electricity and natural gas. It had stakes in nearly 30,000 miles of gas pipeline and a 15,000-mile fiber optic. In 1999, it launched a plan to buy and sell access to high-speed internet bandwidth as well as EnronOnline, a web-based commodity-trading site, making it an e-commerce company. The company reported revenues of $101 billion in 2000 and its stock hit a record high of $90. But in October 2001 Enron reported a $638m third-quarter loss and admitted that the Securities and Exchange Commission had launched a

> **Enron management created a virtual company with virtual profits**

formal investigation into a possible conflict of interest related to the company's dealings with its partners. The next month Enron revised its financial statements for the past five years to account for further losses. Enron shares plunged below $1 and in December it filed for bankruptcy protection. A congressional investigation later concluded that Enron had set up an array of dizzyingly complex schemes to hoodwink the Internal Revenue Service and enrich its executives through tricky accounting off-balance-sheet deals and tax avoidance scams. Enron management created a virtual company with virtual profits. Andrew Fastow pleaded guilty to fraud and agreed to co-operate with prosecutors in return for a 10-year sentence. It remains to be seen whether any other Enron executives will be convicted of a criminal offence and go to jail.

Leading management thinkers

Warren Bennis

A laid-back, silver-haired professor at the University of Southern California who has been a hugely influential authority on leadership for decades, consulted by many of the world's most famous leaders, including at least four American presidents. Bennis's fundamental tenet is that leaders are made, not born. But they should not merely be the best manager around. Being a manager is very different from being a leader. "Managers do things right. Leaders do the right thing," is probably Bennis's most famous quotation.

Managers, however, can learn to be leaders. "I believe in 'possible selves'," Bennis has written, "the capacity to adapt and change." To become good leaders, however, people first have to develop as individuals. Among other things, that involves learning not to be afraid of being seen to be vulnerable. Leadership qualities, he maintains, can only emerge from an "integrated self".

❝❝leaving staff to be entirely self-motivated did not work very well❞❞

Bennis was greatly influenced by Douglas McGregor (see below) and Theory X and Y. In the late 1960s he tried to run the college where he was provost along the lines of Theory Y. But he found in practice that leaving staff to be entirely self-motivated did not work very well. Many people need more structure and direction than McGregor's scheme allowed.

Howard Schultz, the founder and chairman of Starbucks, says that Bennis once told him that in order to become a great leader you have to develop "your ability to leave your own ego at the door, and to recognise the skills and traits that you need in order to build a world-class organisation".

Marvin Bower

For many years the management-consulting business was dominated by one firm. It advised the world's biggest corporations, and indeed the world's biggest countries, about high-level strategy. So outstanding was the firm that it became known simply as "The Firm".

That firm, McKinsey, was the creation of one man. Not James McKinsey, the man whose name hangs over its front door (and who died young of pneumonia in 1938), but Marvin Bower, the most powerful influence on the firm in the 65 years from McKinsey's death to Bower's own, at the age of 99, in 2003.

Bower modelled the consultancy along the lines of a professional law firm. It was driven by a set of values. For example, the clients' interests came before growth in revenue. "If you looked after the client, the profits would look after themselves," Bower wrote in his 1966 book *The Will to Manage*. But he was not afraid to confront clients. One colleague recalls an occasion when Bower "bellowed out, 'The problem with this company, Mr Little, is you.' And there was a deathly silence. It happened to be totally accurate. That was the end of our work with that client, but it didn't bother Marvin."

> **if you looked after the client, the profits would look after themselves**

The Firm's consultants advise top-flight managers. They have been sometimes criticised for not being around to follow through the consequences of their advice. They have a reputation for arrogance. *The Economist* wrote recently of one of them: "He suffers the lack of self-doubt common in former McKinsey consultants." Some of them, such as Tom Peters and Kenichi Ohmae, have gone on to become gurus in their own right.

The Firm itself is organised in an unusual way. It relies heavily on fresh graduates with MBAs or good degrees from top universities to churn the numbers and do the analysis of its clients' problems. These are fed into the "teams" that are put together for each project. The graduates stay only for as long as they continue to progress up the hierarchy. If they stick for too long at one level they are asked to leave. The Firm's policy is "up or out".

Jim Collins

A former professor at the Stanford Business School who found himself with a publishing sensation when he expanded his Stanford research about what it takes to make companies endure into a book. *Built to Last*, published in 1994, allowed Collins to retire from teaching.

Collins excels at the American method of empirical business

leading management thinkers *continued*

research. He gathers masses of data about a group that he wishes to study (in this case, enduringly excellent companies); then he compares it with a "carefully selected" control group that is not enduringly excellent, and sees what are the statistically significant differences. It is a method that takes time, and Collins says that *Built to Last* took six years of research.

His second book, *Good to Great* (2001), has become the best-selling business book of all time, overtaking the long-standing holder of that title, *In Search of Excellence*.

the best students are those who never quite believe their professors

Written after Collins had left Stanford, it took five years of research by 21 assistants at his own "management laboratory" in Boulder, Colorado, near the mountains that he loves to climb. Although Collins can command the highest fees on the business lecture circuit (over $100,000 a day), he prefers to stay close to Boulder.

In a sense, Collins took Peters and Waterman's concept of excellence, and what it is to be an excellent company, and stretched it over time. What does it take to be an excellent company decade after decade?

On his website Collins talks of a professor he knew who walked into his first class and wrote on the board: "The best students are those who never quite believe their professors." What then are we to make of Professor Collins's findings?

W. Edwards Deming

Deming was a statistician who applied ideas about variance from a little-known American mathematician, Walter Shewhart, to business processes – and with dramatic effect in terms of quality and productivity. The surprising thing was that he did it not in his native America, but in Japan. To this day Japanese industry awards a prestigious annual prize (called the Deming Prize) to companies that have demonstrated exceptional improvements in quality.

After the second world war Deming was sent to Japan to advise on a census there. He ended up advising Japanese businessmen how to inject quality into their manufacturing industry, which at the time had a reputation around the world for producing shoddy goods. His secret was to demonstrate that all business processes are vulnerable to a loss of quality through variation. Reduce the variation; increase the quality. Deming once said: "If I had to reduce my message for management to a few words, I'd say it all had to do with reducing variation."

Deming's method for bringing this about was built on what became known as the quality circle (or, in Japan, the Deming circle). This is a group of workers who seek to improve the processes they are responsible for in four stages – through planning how to do it, implementing the plan, checking the variance from anticipated outcomes, and taking action to correct it. Spreading this system throughout an organisation has come to be known as TQM (Total Quality Management), and has been adopted in America as widely as in Japan.

Peter Drucker

The most enduring guru of them all. From his 1946 book, *Concept of the Corporation*, based on his wartime experience as a consultant with General Motors, to his 2004 article ("What Makes an Effective Executive?") in the prestigious *Harvard Business Review* – which won that year's McKinsey prize for the best HBR article of the year – Peter Drucker has never failed to throw light on the tasks and difficulties of management.

> **he has never failed to throw light on the tasks and difficulties of management**

Born in Austria before the first world war, Drucker moved to England in the late 1920s and thence to America in 1937. His academic career did not begin until after the second world war. His interests since have been eclectic. He has invented a quiver of management theories – "management by objectives"; decentralisation; and "structure follows strategy". He coined the phrase "knowledge worker" in 1969. But his focus has always been on the practical – how to make businesses and their managers perform more effectively.

However, Drucker has always set this pragmatic task in a much broader context, and therein lies his enduring appeal. Rosabeth

leading management thinkers *continued*

Moss Kanter, a Harvard academic, once wrote: "In the Drucker perspective ... quality of life, technological progress and world peace are all the products of good management ... at root, Drucker is a management Utopian, descended as much from Robert Owen as Max Weber."

When Jim Collins (see above) was asked what was the best advice he ever received, he said it came from Drucker at a time when Collins was thinking of starting a consulting business rather than pursuing new business ideas. Drucker told him, "The real discipline comes in saying 'no' to the wrong opportunities."

Henri Fayol

While American manufacturing processes were being revolutionised by Taylorism (see below), France's were being overturned by Fayolism, a method devised by an engineer, Henri

❝ he was a great believer in the value of specialisation and the unity of command ❞

Fayol, who rescued a troubled mining company and turned it into one of France's most successful businesses. Fayol's theory was in stark contrast to

Taylor's. He looked for general management principles that could be applied to a wide range of organisations – business, financial or even government. He separated the tasks of management into four categories: planning, organisation, co-ordination and command, and he was a great believer in the value of specialisation and of the unity of command – that each employee should be answerable to only one person.

Fayol remained virtually unknown outside his native France until a quarter of a century after his death (in 1949) when his most important work *General and Industrial Management* – first published in French in 1916 – was finally translated into English. He then became extraordinarily influential as the founding father of what became known as the Administration School of Management. As recently as 1993 he was listed in one poll as the most popular management writer, alongside Douglas McGregor.

Sumantra Ghoshal

A soft-spoken physicist from Calcutta, Ghoshal began his career at Indian Oil and came to management studies with a solid grounding in corporate life. After doctorates at Harvard and MIT, he worked at INSEAD and the London Business School before dying prematurely at the age of 55 in 2004.

Ghoshal's influence far exceeded his written output. He first made his mark in a seminal critique of the widely used matrix form of organisational structure in which managers reported in two directions – along functional lines and along geographic lines. Written in 1990 with his closest collaborator, Christopher

they argued that dual reporting leads to conflict and confusion

Bartlett, the article argued that this dual reporting leads to "conflict and confusion". In large multinationals, "separated by barriers of distance, language, time and culture, managers found it virtually impossible to clarify the confusion and resolve the conflicts".

Bartlett and Ghoshal said that companies needed to alter their organisational psychology (the shared norms and beliefs) and their physiology (the systems that allow information to flow around the organisation) before they start to redesign their anatomy (the reporting lines). Their work set off a search for new metaphors for organisational structures – borrowing in particular from psychology and biology (eg, corporate DNA; the left brain of the organisation).

Shortly before he died, Ghoshal wrote one of his most contentious papers which caused a considerable stir. In it, he suggested that much of the blame for corporate corruption in the early 2000s could be laid at the feet of business schools and the way they taught the MBA degree – a point of view shared by Mintzberg and Bennis.

Gary Hamel

Hamel is perhaps best known for the idea of core competence, a phrase that has spread far beyond the management lexicon. He propounded the idea in a 1990 paper written with an Indian academic, C. K. Prahalad. "Core competencies," they wrote, "are the collective learning in the organisation, especially how to co-ordinate diverse production skills and integrate multiple streams of technologies" – in short, the things an organisation does

leading management thinkers continued

particularly well. This dovetailed with the phenomenon of outsourcing, which allowed companies to hand over to others the processes and operations (such as IT or book-keeping) that were not "core", thus freeing them to concentrate on those things that they did best.

Hamel took corporate strategy away from the precision of traditional planning. He recommended that companies identify their core competencies and then reinvent themselves around that base of knowledge and skill. He saw strategy as a matter of revolution, of dramatic change. Strategic innovation, he said, will be the source of competitive advantage in the future.

> **core competence, a phrase that has spread far beyond the management lexicon**

The brightness of Hamel's star dimmed somewhat in the wake of the Enron collapse. Enron was a company that he had held up as an exemplar of his style of strategic innovation. He had also lauded a number of large Japanese companies whose business model stalled at the end of the 20th century.

Michael Hammer

Hammer was a professor of computer science at MIT who came up with the biggest business idea of the 1990s, re-engineering, which he defined as "the fundamental rethinking and radical redesign of business processes to achieve dramatic improvements in critical measures of performance".

The idea was first propounded in a 1990 *Harvard Business Review* article entitled "Re-engineering Work: Don't Automate, Obliterate". This was followed by a book, *Re-engineering the Corporation*, written with James Champy, the founder of the CSC Index consulting firm. The book sold several million copies.

Hammer marked a symbolic shift from a time when traditional mechanical engineers dominated management thinking to an era in which electronic engineers with computer skills became as influential. Re-engineering was a sort of Taylorism updated to take account of information technology.

So popular was re-engineering that one survey in the 1990s showed it to have been adopted by almost 80% of *Fortune* 500 companies. It was often blamed for the widespread lay-offs that became a part of almost every company's radical redesign of its processes.

Hammer never managed to repeat his success. He opened his own consultancy business and worked on the idea of "the process enterprise". If you really want to make re-engineering successful, he argued, you need a whole new type of organisation.

Charles Handy

An Irish protestant whose broad interests spread from religion and philosophy to the organisation of the workplace. His vivid use of metaphor and accessible writing style have made his books extremely popular – with titles like *The Empty Raincoat* and *The Gods of Management* (in which he identified four different management cultures, which he likens to four Greek Gods: Apollo, Athena, Dionysus and Zeus).

Handy began his career as an employee of the Shell oil company, and was sent to work with a drilling operation in the jungles of Borneo. He later vividly described how little relation his life on the job had to the goal he had been given at headquarters to maximise the company's return on equity. Handy's written work has almost always been a search for ways in which companies can go beyond the pure pursuit of profit. How can they be transformed into communities and soar above being mere properties that are bought and sold?

Handy's academic career began when he went to MIT's Sloan School of Management where, among others, he met Warren Bennis (see above) who, he says, has been his "godfather". He then became a professor at the London Business School where he was responsible for inventing ideas such as the shamrock organisation (which, like the plant, has three leaves – management; specialists; and an increasingly flexible labour force) and portfolio working, a lifestyle in which the individual holds a number of different jobs at the same time.

> **he was responsible for inventing ideas such as the shamrock organisation**

leading management thinkers *continued*

Robert Kaplan

A Harvard professor credited with coming up with two of the most influential management ideas of the late 20th century: activity-based costing (ABC) and the balanced scorecard. The first is an alternative to traditional accounting where overheads (indirect costs) are allocated in proportion to an activity's direct costs. For businesses whose goods are customised, this is not a very accurate method. ABC attempts to improve on it by allocating indirect costs more accurately.

> **activity-based costing (ABC) and the balanced scorecard**

Popular for a while, ABC fell into disrepute when it became clear that it was much simpler in theory than it was in practice.

The concept of the balanced scorecard was developed with David Norton, a consultant. It starts from the idea that with existing systems what you measure is what you get. If you measure only financial performance, then financial performance is the target people aim for. In the balanced scorecard things are measured from a number of different perspectives, not just the financial one – for example, from the customer's perspective, from the company's own internal perspective, and from the perspective of innovation and improvement. How can a company continue to create value in the future? The idea appealed to those managers who felt that traditional measures of performance were unduly focused on shareholders' interests.

Nicolo Machiavelli

The author of one of the most famous books on management ever written, Nicolo Machiavelli remains famous five centuries after the publication of *The Prince*, the short volume in which he outlines what a prince must do to survive and prosper, surrounded as he inevitably will be by general human malevolence. Dedicated to Lorenzo de Medici – the greatest patron of Renaissance art – the book draws on examples such as Alexander the Great and the German city states, to teach its readers eternal lessons about how to stay in power. To this day, there are corporate leaders who keep a copy of *The Prince* by their bedside.

Machiavelli's tripartite division of leaders' tactics – "Some princes, in order to hold on to their states securely, have disarmed their subjects; some have kept their subject towns divided; and some have fostered animosity against themselves" – first expounded in Florence in the 1520s, has been developed into a modern theory about corporate structure.

For a long time Machiavelli's advice was considered amoral and dishonourably scheming. But in the 1860s Victor Hugo reinstated him. "Machiavelli," he wrote, "is not an evil genius, nor a cowardly writer. He is nothing but the fact … not merely the Italian fact, he is the European fact." Now we can say with confidence: he is the global fact.

Abraham Maslow

Maslow is the most influential anthropologist ever to have worked in industry. He lived among the Blackfoot Indians of Alberta, Canada, (where he "found almost the same range of personalities as I find in our society") before becoming a professor of psychology at Brandeis University near Boston, Massachusetts.

The eldest of the seven children of Russian Jewish immigrants to America, Maslow is best known for developing the concept of the hierarchy of needs, a framework for thinking about human motivation. We have five different kinds of needs, he suggested – physiological ones (hunger, thirst and so on); safety needs (job security, risk avoidance, etc); social needs (parties, meetings, family); esteem needs (also called ego needs) such as self-respect, esteem and sense of achievement; and self-actualisation, described by Maslow as: "A musician must make music, an artist must paint, a poet must write, if he is to be ultimately happy. What a man can be, he must be. This need we may call self-actualisation."

he is best known for developing the concept of the hierarchy of needs

Needs in the earlier categories have to be satisfied before needs in the higher ones can act as motivators. (Although the image of the starving poet is a recurring one, and not only in fiction.) Any single act may satisfy more than one need. We have a drink at a bar because we're thirsty and also because we want to meet friends.

leading management thinkers *continued*

Douglas McGregor

A social psychologist by training, McGregor spent most of his relatively short life (he died in 1964 at the age of 58) as an academic at Harvard and MIT. Yet in 1993 he was listed as the most popular management writer ever, alongside the Frenchman Henri Fayol.

McGregor was the first effective counterweight to the mechanistic thinking of Taylor's scientific management. His highly influential idea was expounded in his book *The Human Side of Enterprise*, published in 1960. In it he argued that there are two fundamentally different styles of management. One he called Theory X, an authoritarian style which maintains that management "must counteract an inherent human tendency to avoid work". The other, Theory Y, "assumes that people will exercise self-direction and self-control in the achievement of organisational objectives to the degree that they are committed to those objectives". Management's job is to maximise their commitment.

&& theory Y assumes that people will exercise self-direction and self-control &&

McGregor urged companies to adopt Theory Y. Only it, he believed, could motivate human beings to the highest levels of achievement. His thinking resounds in today's team-based management styles. But McGregor's bifurcated theory has been criticised (by Abraham Maslow, among others) as being tough on the weaker members of society, those who need guidance. Not everyone is sufficiently self-controlled and self-motivated to thrive in a Theory Y environment.

Henry Mintzberg

A consistently contrary Canadian academic who sometimes seems to be undermining the very industry in which he works, Mintzberg first came to fame with a brilliant article in the *Harvard Business Review* in 1975 entitled "The Manager's Job: Folklore and Fact". He studied what a number of managers in different industrial sectors actually did, day in, day out. And he found that

"Jumping from topic to topic, he (the manager) thrives on interruptions and more often than not disposes of items in ten minutes or less. Though he may have 50 projects going, all are delegated." A sample of British managers were found to work for more than half an hour without interruption "about once every two days". So much for careful strategic planning.

In *Managers not MBAs*, published in 2004, Mintzberg argued that the MBA, the bread-and-butter course of many business schools, and the *sine qua non* of fast-track management careers, "prepares people to manage nothing". Synthesis, not analysis, he says, "is the very essence of management", and MBA courses teach only analysis. Failed leaders such as Ford's Robert McNamara and Enron's Jeffrey Skilling, who came near the top of their class at Harvard Business School, were star MBA students and brilliant analysts. That was not enough, however, to turn them into great managers or leaders.

Kenichi Ohmae

The only management guru of any stature to have emerged from Japan. Trained as a nuclear physicist at MIT, Ohmae was head of McKinsey's Tokyo office when he published his most famous book, *Triad Power*, in 1985. At a time when multinational firms were busily spreading their operations around the world, he argued that they needed to be strong in all three major economic blocs – Europe, North America and the Pacific Rim, "the Triad" – if they were to compete successfully against others who were strong in those places.

> **the difference between Japanese firms and their western counterparts is their time frame**

Ohmae was also influential in spreading the idea that the major difference between Japanese firms and their western counterparts is their time frame. Japanese firms look to the longer-term, while western firms, driven by the demands of their stockmarkets, are more focused on short-term profits. He argued that this short-term focus led western companies to pay too little attention to their customers. "In the long run," he wrote, "the corporation that is genuinely interested in its customers is the one that will be interesting to investors."

Ohmae's books are full of Japanese examples and they helped

leading management thinkers *continued*

familiarise western audiences with Japan's management breakthroughs – for example, the introduction of the just-in-time (JIT) system at Toyota. Ohmae tells how it came about because one worker, Taiichi Ohno, continually asked why the company needed to (expensively) stockpile vast quantities of components for its production line.

Tom Peters

Tom Peters was the co-author of what was, for over 20 years, the best-selling business book of all time. *In Search of Excellence*, written with his fellow McKinsey consultant, Robert Waterman, was first published in 1987 and has sold millions of copies. Part of its success lay in capturing the zeitgeist of the times. Corporate America was feeling overwhelmed by Japan's evident superiority in manufacturing. It needed a reminder that there were still excellent businesses in the United States.

> **a bias for action, sticking to their knitting, and staying close to their customers**

Peters and Waterman identified 43 American companies out of the *Fortune* 500 that had consistently outperformed the average over a 20-year period. They then identified a number of features these companies had in common – including a bias for action, sticking to their knitting and staying close to their customers.

After the book was published, the two authors went their separate ways. Peters became an energetic speaker on the business circuit, earnings tens of thousands of dollars per performance. The more retiring Waterman set up his own consultancy. They never wrote another book together although each separately wrote several. Peters's 1987 book *Thriving on Chaos* begins with the memorable line: "There are no excellent companies."

The focus of Peters's later work is the managament of continuous change in a chaotic world. His books became ever more popular. *Re-imagine*, published in 2003 by Dorling Kindersley, a publisher famous for its artwork, contains lots of sidebars, exclamation marks and pictures of things like frogs leaping.

Michael Porter

Michael Porter redefined the way that businessmen think about competition. He began by simplifying the notion of competitive advantage and then created a new framework for companies to think about how to achieve it.

Competitive advantage, he wrote, is "a function of either providing comparable buyer value more efficiently than competitors (low cost) or performing activities at comparable cost, but in unique ways that create more buyer value than competitors and, hence, command a premium price (differentiation)".

Porter maintained that there are five forces driving competition in business:

- existing rivalry between firms;
- the threat of a new entrant to a market;
- the threat of substitute products and services;
- the bargaining power of suppliers;
- the bargaining power of buyers.

Like many leading management thinkers, from Frederick Taylor on, Porter trained first as an engineer. But after a doctorate in economics he became a professor at Harvard Business School. Like Tom Peters, he is a skilful presenter who commands high fees on the lecture circuit.

In his book *Competitive Advantage* (1985), Porter introduced the idea of the value chain, which has been highly influential in subsequent strategic thinking. He created a model in which the firm is structured as a chain of value-creating activities. The chain is divided into five main links – inbound logistics, operations, outbound logistics, marketing and sales, and services.

> the firm is structured as a chain of value-creating activities

In his later work Porter looked at ways in which nations gain competitive advantage over each other, and this led him to focus on the phenomenon of clustering. Nations did well, he maintained, in large part because of the accumulation of specialised skills and industries that, through dynamic competition between them, brought about superior products and processes.

Leading management thinkers

leading management thinkers *continued*

Frederick Winslow Taylor

A true pioneer, Taylor was, in Peter Drucker's words, "the first man in history who did not take work for granted, but looked at it and studied it. His approach to work is still

the basic foundation." Taylor trained as an engineer but then worked as a manager at the Midvale Steel Works in Philadelphia. There he took to walking around with a stop-watch and a notepad breaking down manual tasks into a series of components and thereby measuring the workers' productivity. Out of this grew the idea of piece work.

Taylor's first book, *A Piece-Rate System*, was published in 1895. A later publication made him the author of the very first business

Lenin exhorted workers to 'try out every scientific and progressive suggestion of the Taylor system'

bestseller, *The Principles of Scientific Management*, published in 1911. Its influence spread to unlikely places. Lenin at one time exhorted Soviet workers to "try out every scientific and progressive suggestion of the Taylor system". Subsequent failure to achieve Taylor-like production targets led many Soviet workers to the gulag.

Today, scientific management – sometimes called "Taylorism" – is often seen as representing the dehumanising aspect of industrialisation, a system that has no room for the nuances of human nature as it surges on to find the one best way.

Sun Tzu

The ultimate military strategist, Sun Tzu was a general who lived in China over 2,400 years ago whose victories would be no more recalled than those of many other military leaders had he not put down his thoughts in a slim tome (of a mere 25 pages of text). Called in the original Chinese, *The Military Method of Mr Sun*, today the book is better known as *The Art of War*.

The Art of War contains much wisdom of relevance today. For example, Sun Tzu asks: "Why destroy when you can win by stealth and cunning?" His fundamental strategy is a bit like that of judo: undermine your enemy by using the power of his own momentum against him.

Gary Hamel (see above) put Sun Tzu in his proper place when he wrote: "Strategy didn't start with Igor Ansoff, neither did it start with Machiavelli. It probably did not even start with Sun Tzu. Strategy is as old as human conflict."

> **why destroy when you can win by stealth and cunning**

Nevertheless, *The Art of War* is still almost compulsory reading for businessmen in the east. Sun Tzu's advice to businessmen in the west would probably be: "To beat your enemies, first know their strategy – or at least where they are likely to be getting that strategy from."

The oldest stock exchanges

Exchange	City	Founding year
Amsterdam Stock Exchange	Amsterdam	1602
Paris Bourse	Paris	1724
Philadelphia Stock Exchange	Philadelphia	1790
London Stock Exchange	London	1801*
Milan Stock Exchange	Milan	1808
New York Stock Exchange	New York	1817†
Frankfurt Stock Exchange	Frankfurt	1820‡
Bolsa de Madrid	Madrid	1831
Toronto Stock Exchange	Toronto	1861
Australian Stock Exchange	Sydney	1872
Bombay Stock Exchange	Mumbai	1875
Zurich Stock Exchange	Zurich	1877
Tokyo Stock Exchange	Tokyo	1878
Chicago Stock Exchange	Chicago	1882
Pacific Stock Exchange	San Francisco	1882
Johannesburg Stock Exchange	Johannesburg	1887
Bovespa	São Paulo	1890
Hong Kong Stock Exchange	Hong Kong	1891
Cairo Stock Exchange	Cairo	1903
Istanbul Stock Exchange	Istanbul	1929**
Mercado de Valores (Merval)	Buenos Aires	1929
NASDAQ	United States	1971
Stock Exchange of Singapore	Singapore	1973

Note: Amsterdam is not the only exchange claiming to be the oldest but it does seem to have been the first established stock exchange.
*Preceded by Johnathan's Coffee House, records beginning 1698
†Preceded by the Buttonwood Agreement, signed 1792
‡First share issue traded; had existed as bond exchange since late 18th century
**Originally Istanbul Securities and Foreign Exchange Bourse

Leading stockmarkets

Total market capitalisation, 2004, $bn		Total value traded, 2004, $bn	
US	16,324	US	19,355
Japan	3,678	UK	3,707
UK	2,816	Japan	3,430
France	1,857	Germany	1,406
Germany	1,195	France	1,312
Canada	1,178	Spain	1,195
Spain	941	Italy	804
Hong Kong	861	China	748
Switzerland	826	Switzerland	727
Italy	790	Taiwan	719
Australia	776	Canada	654
Belgium	768	South Korea	639
China	640	Netherlands	604
Netherlands	622	Australia	514
South Africa	456	Saudi Arabia	473
Taiwan	441	Hong Kong	439
South Korea	429	Sweden	412
India	388	India	379
Sweden	377	Finland	220
Brazil	330	South Africa	163
Saudi Arabia	306	Turkey	147
Russia	268	Norway	135
Malaysia	190	Russia	131
Finland	184	Thailand	110
Mexico	172	Denmark	97
Singapore	172	Brazil	94
Denmark	151	Singapore	81
Norway	141	Pakistan	74
Greece	125	Belgium	70
Chile	117	Malaysia	60
Thailand	115	Israel	46
Ireland	114	Ireland	44
Turkey	98	Greece	43
Israel	96	Mexico	43
Austria	86	Portugal	35
Portugal	73	Indonesia	28
Indonesia	73	Austria	24
Poland	71	Czech Republic	18
Luxembourg	50	Poland	17
Iran	47	New Zealand	15

Source: Standard & Poor's

Some stockmarket indices explained

CAC 40 Index

The CAC 40 is France's benchmark index for the Paris Bourse. CAC stands for "*Cotation Assistée en Continu*", or "continuous-time computer-assisted quotation". The index comprises the 40 biggest companies on the Paris Bourse. It has a base value of 1,000 starting on December 31st 1987. The index is reviewed quarterly.

DAX 30 Index

The DAX (Deutsche Aktienindex) 30 is composed of Germany's 30 largest and most liquid listed companies. Its base value is 1,000 starting on December 31st 1987. Unlike most stock indices, the DAX includes dividend calculations and thus is a measure of total returns, not just price performance.

Dow Jones Industrial Average Index

The Dow Jones Company started tracking an index of 12 industrial companies' stock prices on May 26th 1896. It now comprises 30 stocks which are no longer necessarily in the industrial sector. The index is price-weighted, rather than market-capitalisation weighted, unlike most major stock indices. Also unlike most other indices, its component companies change irregularly and rarely, and changes are based not on specific criteria but the judgment of editors of the *Wall Street Journal*. It is the most quoted stockmarket index in print, television and internet media.

FTSE Actuaries All-Share Index and FTSE 100 Index

The FTSE ("Footsie") indices derive their name from the acronym for the "Financial Times Stock Exchange" index. The All-Share index was first calculated in 1962. The more closely followed FSTE 100 index began on January 3rd 1984, with a value of 1,000. It includes the top 100 listed firms by market capitalisation on the London Stock Exchange and is reviewed quarterly. The FTSE 250, created in 1985, represents mid-capitalisation companies in Britain not covered by the FTSE 100 and has become increasingly popular in recent years.

Hang Seng Index

The Hang Seng Index derives its name from Hong Kong's Hang Seng Bank, which created the index in 1969. Optimistically, "Hang Seng" means "ever-growing" in Chinese. It comprises the 33 largest companies drawn from four industry groups, and accounts for about 70% of the Hong Kong stockmarket's value. The index's base value is 100, corresponding to August 1964.

NASDAQ Composite Index

NASDAQ is the acronym for the National Association of Securities Dealers Automated Quotations system. The NASDAQ Composite index tracks the performance of all stocks traded on the NASDAQ exchange system, currently over 3,000. The NASDAQ is dominated by technology firms, so the performance of the NASDAQ Composite is closely watched as a barometer for the information-technology industry.

Nikkei 225 Index

The Nikkei 225 is Japan's most closely watched stock index, published by the business daily *Neihon Keizai Shimbun* (*Nikkei*). It measures the performance of 225 of the top stocks on the Tokyo Stock Exchange. Established on September 7th 1950, but with a base value of 100 starting on May 16th 1949, it is a price-based index like the Dow Jones Industrial Average. It is reviewed at least once a year but only a maximum of six stocks can be replaced each year.

Standard & Poor's 500 Index

Standard & Poor's, a credit-rating agency and provider of securities research, created the S&P 500 index in 1957. However, its base value of 10 represents the average value of its components from 1941 to 1943. The index is designed to reflect the performance of the largest US companies by market capitalisation, but by virtue of the number of constituents, to a significant degree it reflects the market as a whole. It is reviewed at least once a month.

Stockmarket *performance*

| Year | UK | | | | US |
| | FTSE All Share | | FTSE 100 | | S&P 500 |
	Index	% change	Index	% change	Index
1969	147.3				92.1
1970	136.3	-7.5			92.2
1971	193.4	41.9			102.1
1972	218.2	12.8			118.1
1973	149.8	-31.4			97.6
1974	66.9	-55.3			68.6
1975	158.1	136.3			90.2
1976	152.0	-3.9			107.5
1977	214.5	41.2			95.1
1978	220.2	2.7	484.2		96.1
1979	229.8	4.3	509.2	5.2	107.9
1980	292.2	27.2	647.4	27.1	135.8
1981	313.1	7.2	684.3	5.7	122.6
1982	382.2	22.1	834.3	21.9	140.6
1983	470.5	23.1	1,000.0	19.9	164.9
1984	592.9	26.0	1,232.2	23.2	167.2
1985	682.9	15.2	1,412.6	14.6	211.3
1986	835.5	22.3	1,679.0	18.9	242.2
1987	870.2	4.2	1,712.7	2.0	247.1
1988	926.6	6.5	1,793.1	4.7	277.7
1989	1,204.7	30.0	2,422.7	35.1	353.4
1990	1,032.3	-14.3	2,143.5	-11.5	330.2
1991	1,187.7	15.1	2,493.1	16.3	417.1
1992	1,363.8	14.8	2,846.5	14.2	435.7
1993	1,682.2	23.3	3,418.4	20.1	466.5
1994	1,521.4	-9.6	3,065.5	-10.3	459.3
1995	1,803.1	18.5	3,689.3	20.3	615.9
1996	2,013.7	11.7	4,118.5	11.6	740.7
1997	2,411.0	19.7	5,135.5	24.7	970.4
1998	2,673.9	10.9	5,882.6	14.5	1,229.2
1999	3,242.1	21.2	6,930.2	17.8	1,469.3
2000	2,983.8	-8.0	6,222.5	-10.2	1,320.3
2001	2,523.9	-15.4	5,217.4	-16.2	1,148.1
2002	1,893.7	-25.0	3,940.4	-24.5	879.8
2003	2,207.4	16.6	4,476.9	13.6	1,111.9
2004	2,410.8	9.2	4,814.3	7.5	1,211.9
1969–2004 %		1,669.2		na	
1989–2004 %		133.5		124.6	
Performance since:		1969		1978	
Compound growth %		8.3		9.2	
Average change %		11.8		10.2	
Standard deviation %		29.5		14.6	

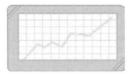

| | US | | | | | Japan | | |
S&P 500 % change	Dow Jones Index	Dow Jones % change	NASDAQ 100 Index	NASDAQ 100 % change	Nikkei 225 Index	Nikkei 225 % change	Topix Index	Topix % change
	800.4				2,348.0		177.8	
0.1	838.9	4.8			1,987.1	-15.4	148.4	-16.6
10.8	890.2	6.1			2,713.7	36.6	199.5	34.4
15.6	1,020.0	14.6			5,207.9	91.9	401.7	101.4
-17.4	850.9	-16.6			4,306.8	-17.3	306.4	-23.7
-29.7	616.2	-27.6			3,836.9	-10.9	278.7	-9.0
31.5	852.4	38.3			4,342.1	13.2	321.8	15.5
19.1	1,004.7	17.9			4,990.9	14.9	383.9	19.3
-11.5	831.2	-17.3			4,865.6	-2.5	364.1	-5.2
1.1	805.0	-3.1			6,001.9	23.4	449.6	23.5
12.3	838.7	4.2			6,569.5	9.5	459.6	2.2
25.8	964.0	14.9			7,063.1	7.5	491.1	6.9
-9.7	875.0	-9.2			7,681.8	8.8	570.3	16.1
14.8	1,046.5	19.6			8,016.7	4.4	593.7	4.1
17.3	1,258.6	20.3	133.1		9,893.8	23.4	731.8	23.3
1.4	1,211.6	-3.7	108.6	-18.4	11,542.6	16.7	913.4	24.8
26.3	1,546.7	27.7	132.3	21.8	13,083.2	13.3	1,047.1	14.6
14.6	1,896.0	22.6	141.4	6.9	18,820.7	43.9	1,562.6	49.2
2.0	1,938.8	2.3	156.3	10.5	21,564.0	14.6	1,725.8	10.4
12.4	2,168.6	11.8	177.4	13.5	30,159.0	39.9	2,357.0	36.6
27.3	2,753.2	27.0	223.8	26.2	38,915.9	29.0	2,881.4	22.2
-6.6	2,633.7	-4.3	200.5	-10.4	23,848.7	-38.7	1,733.8	-39.8
26.3	3,168.8	20.3	330.9	65.0	22,983.8	-3.6	1,714.7	-1.1
4.5	3,301.1	4.2	360.2	8.9	16,925.0	-26.4	1,307.7	-23.7
7.1	3,754.1	13.7	398.3	10.6	17,417.2	2.9	1,439.3	10.1
-1.5	3,834.4	2.1	404.3	1.5	19,723.1	13.2	1,559.1	8.3
34.1	5,117.1	33.5	576.2	42.5	19,868.2	0.7	1,577.7	1.2
20.3	6,448.3	26.0	821.4	42.5	19,361.4	-2.6	1,470.9	-6.8
31.0	7,908.2	22.6	990.8	20.6	15,258.7	-21.2	1,175.0	-20.1
26.7	9,181.4	16.1	1,836.0	85.3	13,842.2	-9.3	1,087.0	-7.5
19.5	11,497.1	25.2	3,707.8	101.9	18,934.3	36.8	1,722.2	58.4
-10.1	10,786.9	-6.2	2,341.7	-36.8	13,785.7	-27.2	1,283.7	-25.5
-13.0	10,021.5	-7.1	1,577.1	-32.7	10,542.6	-23.5	1,032.1	-19.6
-23.4	8,341.6	-16.8	984.4	-37.6	8,579.0	-18.6	843.3	-18.3
26.4	10,453.9	25.3	1,467.9	49.1	10,676.6	24.5	1,043.7	23.8
9.0	10,783.0	3.1	1,621.1	10.4	11,488.8	7.6	1,149.6	10.2
1,215.2		1,185.3		na		478.2		674.9
267.0		309.4		708.4		-51.8		-33.7
1969		1969		1983		1969		1969
7.6		7.7		12.6		4.6		5.5
9.0		8.9		18.2		7.4		8.6
16.7		16.1		37.1		25.4		27.3

Stockmarket performance

| | Hong Kong Hang Seng | | Canada TSE 300 | | Germany Dax 30 | | France CAC 40 |
	Index	% change	Index	% change	Index	% change	Index
1969	155.5		1,053.2		622.4		
1970	211.6	36.1	985.8	-6.4	443.9	-28.7	
1971	341.4	61.3	1,026.5	4.1	473.5	6.7	
1972	843.4	147.1	1,252.2	22.0	536.4	13.3	
1973	433.7	-48.6	1,207.5	-3.6	396.3	-26.1	
1974	171.1	-60.5	885.9	-26.6	401.8	1.4	
1975	350.0	104.5	973.8	9.9	563.3	40.2	
1976	447.7	27.9	1,012.1	3.9	509.0	-9.6	
1977	404.0	-9.8	1,059.6	4.7	549.3	7.9	
1978	495.5	22.6	1,310.0	23.6	575.2	4.7	
1979	879.4	77.5	1,813.2	38.4	497.8	-13.5	
1980	1,473.6	67.6	2,268.7	25.1	480.9	-3.4	
1981	1,405.8	-4.6	1,954.2	-13.9	490.4	2.0	
1982	783.8	-44.2	1,958.1	0.2	552.8	12.7	
1983	874.9	11.6	2,552.3	30.3	774.0	40.0	
1984	1,200.4	37.2	2,400.3	-6.0	820.9	6.1	
1985	1,752.5	46.0	2,900.6	20.8	1,366.2	66.4	
1986	2,568.3	46.6	3,066.2	5.7	1,432.3	4.8	
1987	2,302.8	-10.3	3,160.1	3.1	1,000.0	-30.2	1,000.0
1988	2,687.4	16.7	3,390.0	7.3	1,327.9	32.8	1,573.9
1989	2,836.6	5.5	3,969.8	17.1	1,790.4	34.8	2,001.1
1990	3,024.6	6.6	3,256.8	-18.0	1,398.2	-21.9	1,517.9
1991	4,297.3	42.1	3,512.4	7.8	1,578.0	12.9	1,765.7
1992	5,512.4	28.3	3,350.4	-4.6	1,545.1	-2.1	1,857.8
1993	11,888.4	115.7	4,321.4	29.0	2,266.7	46.7	2,268.2
1994	8,191.0	-31.1	4,213.6	-2.5	2,106.6	-7.1	1,881.2
1995	10,073.4	23.0	4,713.5	11.9	2,253.9	7.0	1,872.0
1996	13,451.5	33.5	5,927.0	25.7	2,888.7	28.2	2,315.7
1997	10,722.8	-20.3	6,699.4	13.0	4,249.7	47.1	2,998.9
1998	10,048.6	-6.3	6,485.9	-3.2	5,002.4	17.7	3,942.7
1999	16,962.1	68.8	8,413.8	29.7	6,958.1	39.1	5,958.3
2000	15,095.5	-11.0	8,933.7	6.2	6,433.6	-7.5	5,926.4
2001	11,397.2	-24.5	7,688.4	-13.9	5,160.1	-19.8	4,624.6
2002	9,321.3	-18.2	6,614.5	-14.0	2,892.6	-43.9	3,063.9
2003	12,575.9	34.9	8,220.9	24.3	3,965.2	37.1	3,557.9
2004	14,230.1	13.2	9,246.7	12.5	4,256.1	7.3	3,821.2
1969–2004 %		6,623.7		838.0		858.9	
1989–2004 %		370.5		132.9		137.7	
Performance since:		1969		1969		1969	
Compound growth %		13.8		6.4		5.6	
Average change %		22.4		7.5		8.7	
Standard deviation %		46.2		15.7		25.5	

Source: Thomson Datastream

France CAC40	Italy BCI		Spain Madrid General		Australia All Share		Emerging markets MSCI Emg Mkts Free	
% change	Index	% change	Index	% change	Index	% change	Index	% change
	106.5							
	75.8	-28.9	115.2					
	77.8	2.6	119.9	4.0				
	78.3	0.7	82.3	-31.3				
	69.3	-11.5	55.4	-32.8				
	96.5	39.3	49.5	-10.6				
	103.8	7.6	41.9	-15.4				
	221.1	113.0	44.4	6.1				
	278.1	25.8	55.1	24.0				
	267.9	-3.7	45.1	-18.2				
	314.6	17.4	52.5	16.5				
	392.4	24.7	73.9	40.7				
	792.6	102.0	100.0	35.3				
	1,454.1	83.5	208.3	108.3				
	982.5	-32.4	227.2	9.1			100.0	
57.4	1,202.5	22.4	274.4	20.8			134.9	34.9
27.1	1,312.8	9.2	296.8	8.2			214.7	59.2
-24.1	939.4	-28.4	223.3	-24.8			185.2	-13.8
16.3	977.4	4.0	246.2	10.3			288.8	56.0
5.2	962.7	-1.5	214.3	-13.0	1,589.1		314.9	9.0
22.1	1,433.1	48.9	322.8	50.7	2,153.3	35.5	539.3	71.3
-17.1	1,443.6	0.7	285.0	-11.7	1,891.7	-12.1	492.6	-8.7
-0.5	1,410.7	-2.3	320.1	12.3	2,188.5	15.7	458.4	-6.9
23.7	1,574.5	11.6	444.8	39.0	2,404.8	9.9	476.3	3.9
29.5	2,508.8	59.3	632.6	42.2	2,579.5	7.3	412.5	-13.4
31.5	3,548.7	41.4	867.8	37.2	2,697.0	4.6	299.0	-27.5
51.1	4,342.6	22.4	1,008.6	16.2	3,108.8	15.3	489.4	63.7
-0.5	4,426.2	1.9	880.7	-12.7	3,154.7	1.5	333.8	-31.8
-22.0	3,261.6	-26.3	824.4	-6.4	3,359.9	6.5	317.4	-4.9
-33.7	2,416.2	-25.9	634.0	-23.1	2,975.4	-11.4	292.1	-8.0
16.1	2,715.0	12.4	808.0	27.4	3,306.0	11.1	442.8	51.6
7.4	3,153.7	16.2	959.1	18.7	4,053.1	22.6	542.2	22.4
na		na		na		na		na
91.0		140.2		223.1		na		152.5
1987		1973		1974		1993		1988
8.2		11.5		7.3		8.1		10.5
11.1		16.3		10.9		8.9		15.1
25.7		35.8		29.8		13.2		34.2

$tockmarkets: the best and worst of times

MSCI World Index

Best days				Worst days			
Date	Close	Change, points	Change, %	Date	Close	Change, points	Change, %
21/10/87	418.89	32.47	8.40	19/10/87	421.28	-46.00	-9.84
29/7/02	821.13	39.08	5.00	20/10/87	386.42	-34.87	-8.28
17/1/91	460.54	21.45	4.88	26/10/87	378.35	-24.05	-5.98
30/10/87	402.28	15.33	3.96	19/8/91	472.32	-25.26	-5.08
2/10/90	446.82	16.98	3.95	27/10/97	893.91	-41.34	-4.42
24/9/01	888.68	32.09	3.75	14/4/00	1,329.98	-54.08	-3.91
29/9/81	138.60	4.80	3.59	22/7/02	776.93	-29.21	-3.62
10/4/92	484.71	15.76	3.36	12/3/01	1093.10	-40.65	-3.59
27/8/90	469.20	14.89	3.28	17/3/80	124.40	-4.60	-3.57
16/3/00	1,392.79	44.18	3.28	19/7/02	806.14	-29.00	-3.47

MSCI World Index

Best years				Worst years			
Year	Close	Change, points	Change, %	Year	Close	Change, points	Change, %
1933	22.29	9.02	68.02	1931	13.48	-9.40	-41.08
1986	356.83	100.31	39.11	1920	14.98	-6.51	-30.28
1954	38.25	10.60	38.33	1974	78.24	-30.17	-27.83
1985	256.51	69.31	37.02	1930	22.89	-7.63	-25.00
1958	52.34	12.06	29.95	1946	22.73	-6.22	-21.47
1975	100.86	22.63	28.92	1990	461.53	-105.81	-18.65
1959	66.73	14.39	27.49	2001	1,003.52	-217.73	-17.83
1999	1,420.88	270.93	23.56	1937	24.81	-5.13	-17.13
1998	1,149.95	213.36	22.78	1973	108.41	-22.33	-17.08
1980	159.20	28.40	21.71	2000	1,221.25	-199.63	-14.05

Source: Global Financial Data
(www.globalfinancialdata.com)

US S&P 500 Index

Best days				Worst days			
Date	Close	Change, points	Change, %	Date	Close	Change, points	Change, %
15/3/33	6.81	0.97	16.60	19/10/87	224.84	-57.86	-20.47
30/10/29	22.99	2.56	12.53	28/10/29	22.74	-3.20	-12.34
6/10/31	9.91	1.10	12.43	29/10/29	20.43	-2.31	-10.16
21/9/32	8.51	0.89	11.74	6/11/29	20.61	-2.19	-9.61
5/9/39	12.64	1.11	9.61	18/10/37	10.76	-1.11	-9.34
20/4/33	7.82	0.68	9.52	20/7/33	10.57	-1.03	-8.90
21/10/87	258.38	21.55	9.10	21/7/33	9.65	-0.92	-8.70
14/11/29	19.24	1.58	8.95	26/10/87	227.67	-20.55	-8.28
3/8/32	6.39	0.52	8.80	5/10/32	7.39	-0.66	-8.14
8/10/31	10.62	0.83	8.49	12/8/32	7.00	-0.62	-8.10

US S&P 500 Index

Best years				Worst years			
Year	Close	Change, points	Change, %	Year	Close	Change, points	Change, %
1862	2.63	0.94	55.36	1931	8.12	-7.22	-47.04
1933	10.10	3.21	46.62	1937	10.54	-6.64	-38.64
1954	35.99	11.17	45.03	1907	6.57	-3.27	-33.23
1843	2.33	0.72	45.02	1857	1.48	-0.67	-30.99
1879	4.92	1.48	42.96	1917	6.80	-3.00	-30.61
1935	13.44	3.94	41.51	1854	2.03	-0.88	-30.21
1958	55.21	15.22	38.06	1974	68.56	-28.99	-29.72
1863	3.63	1.00	38.01	1930	15.34	-6.11	-28.48
1928	24.35	6.69	37.88	1920	6.81	-2.21	-24.51
1908	9.03	2.46	37.44	1893	4.41	-1.10	-19.96

Source: Global Financial Data (www.globalfinancialdata.com)

Note: These calculations are based on monthly data 1800–1917; weekly data 1918–27; daily data from 1928.

stockmarkets: best and worst times *continued*

Financial Times 30 Industrials

Best days				Worst days			
Date	Close	Change, points	Change, %	Date	Close	Change, points	Change, %
23/9/31	56.89	6.46	12.81	20/10/87	951.95	-120.45	-11.23
24/1/75	91.29	7.81	9.36	19/10/87	1,072.40	-117.52	-9.88
10/2/75	117.53	9.31	8.60	1/3/74	138.40	-10.87	-7.28
29/9/38	79.90	6.20	8.41	26/10/87	863.73	-66.60	-7.16
30/1/75	106.22	7.13	7.20	29/5/62	261.30	-18.00	-6.44
7/2/75	108.22	6.36	6.24	2/1/75	62.60	-4.29	-6.41
30/3/71	352.20	20.50	6.18	31/1/75	236.90	-15.40	-6.10
27/1/75	96.88	5.59	6.12	17/3/75	291.70	-17.80	-5.75
9/10/59	284.70	16.10	5.99	8/11/76	291.00	-17.70	-5.73
10/4/92	1,232.15	68.24	5.86	11/2/75	260.70	-15.20	-5.51

Financial Times All Share Index

Best years				Worst years			
Year	Close	Change, points	Change, %	Year	Close	Change, points	Change, %
1975	158.08	91.19	136.33	1974	66.89	-82.87	-55.34
1824	45.53	21.65	90.67	1721	20.42	-10.11	-33.12
1959	106.93	32.36	43.39	1973	149.76	-68.42	-31.36
1971	193.39	57.13	41.93	1705	13.51	-4.20	-23.72
1977	214.53	62.57	41.18	1931	21.83	-6.69	-23.46
1968	168.60	46.42	37.99	1825	35.17	-10.35	-22.74
1954	62.66	16.07	34.48	1866	20.89	-6.04	-22.42
1958	74.57	18.59	33.20	1803	16.60	-4.66	-21.92
1817	19.13	4.71	32.62	1694	16.63	-4.34	-20.70
1967	122.18	29.70	32.12	1826	28.10	-7.07	-20.10

Source: Global Financial Data (www.globalfinancialdata.com)

Japan Topix Price Index

Best days				Worst days			
Date	Close	Change, points	Change, %	Date	Close	Change, points	Change, %
2/10/90	1,668.83	145.40	9.54	20/10/87	1,793.90	-307.27	-14.62
21/10/87	1,962.41	168.51	9.39	5/3/53	32.32	-3.10	-8.75
21/8/92	1,251.70	87.93	7.56	30/4/70	159.33	-12.86	-7.47
10/4/92	1,282.56	86.37	7.22	2/4/90	2,069.33	-158.15	-7.10
17/11/97	1,257.85	80.33	6.82	12/9/01	990.80	-67.32	-6.36
31/1/94	1,629.22	101.40	6.64	17/4/00	1,552.46	-101.24	-6.12
6/1/88	1,820.03	112.14	6.57	30/3/53	30.31	-1.93	-5.99
16/4/53	32.79	1.97	6.39	16/8/71	196.99	-12.01	-5.75
21/3/01	1,275.41	75.80	6.32	23/8/90	1,829.25	-110.58	-5.70
6/3/53	34.06	1.74	5.38	19/8/91	1,663.94	-92.00	-5.24

Japan Topix Price Index

Best years				Worst years			
Year	Close	Change, points	Change, %	Year	Close	Change, points	Change, %
1952	32.20	17.46	118.38	1920	2.44	-2.33	-48.83
1972	401.70	202.25	101.40	1990	1,733.83	-1,147.54	-39.83
1932	2.69	1.25	86.31	1946	2.55	-1.05	-29.13
1948	6.47	2.98	85.28	2000	1,283.67	-438.53	-25.46
1951	14.75	5.70	62.95	1992	1,307.66	-407.02	-23.74
1999	1,722.20	635.21	58.44	1973	306.44	-95.26	-23.71
1915	2.85	0.98	52.01	1930	1.49	-0.40	-21.09
1949	9.76	3.29	50.89	1997	1,175.03	-295.91	-20.12
1986	1,556.37	506.97	48.31	2001	1,032.14	-251.53	-19.59
1958	60.95	17.55	40.44	1970	148.35	-30.95	-17.26

Source: Global Financial Data (www.globalfinancialdata.com)

Clocking the stockmarkets

DST factor:January GMT +/–		−5	−2	+0	+1
When the			*the time in*		
market	Local	New	São	London	Frankfurt
opens in:	opening	York	Paulo		
	times		*is*		
New York	9:30	9:30	12:30	14:30	15:30
São Paulo	11:00	8:00	11:00	13:00	14:00
London	8:00	3:00	6:00	8:00	9:00
Frankfurt	9:00	8:00	6:00	8:00	9:00
Bombay	10:00	14:30	2:30	4:30	5:30
Singapore	9:00	18:00	21:00	1:00	2:00
Hong Kong	10:00	17:00	20:00	2:00	3:00
Tokyo	9:00	19:00	22:00	0:00	1:00
Sydney	10:00	18:00	21:00	23:00	0:00

Sources: Stock exchanges; *The Economist* diary

+5.5	+8	+8	+9	+11
		the time in		
Bombay	Singapore	Hong Kong	Tokyo	Sydney
		is		
20:00	22:30	22:30	23:30	1:30
18:30	21:00	21:00	22:00	0:00
13:30	16:00	16:00	17:00	19:00
13:30	16:00	16:00	17:00	19:00
10:00	12:30	12:30	13:30	15:30
6:30	9:00	9:00	10:00	12:00
7:30	10:00	10:00	11:00	13:00
5:30	8:00	8:00	9:00	11:00
4:30	7:00	7:00	8:00	10:00

Bonds

Credit ratings

	Moody's	Standard & Poor's
Highest credit quality; issuer has strong ability to meet obligations	Aaa	AAA
Very high credit quality; low risk of default	Aa1, Aa2, Aa3	AA+, AA, AA-
High credit quality, but more vulnerable to changes in economy or busines	A1, A2, A3	A+, A, A-
Adequate credit quality for now but more likely to be impaired if conditions worsen	Baa1, Baa2, Baa3	BBB+, BBB, BBB-
Below investment grade, but good chance that issuer can meet commitments	Ba1, Ba2, Ba3	BB+, BB, BB-
Significant credit risk, but issuer is currently able to meet obligations	B1, B2, B3	B+, B, B-
High default risk	Caa1, Caa2, Caa3	CCC+, CCC, CCC-
Issuer failed to meet scheduled interest or principal payments	C	D

Source: *Guide to Financial Markets* by Marc Levinson, The Economist/Profile Books

US corporate bonds, issuance, $bn

	High yield	Investment grade	Total
1990	10.8	142.7	153.5
1991	13.3	202.2	215.5
1992	42.4	247.6	290.0
1993	72.8	322.9	395.7
1994	45.4	230.1	275.5
1995	43.3	273.9	317.2
1996	70.9	338.0	408.9
1997	131.2	425.1	556.3
1998	144.5	564.1	708.6
1999	97.0	657.4	754.4
2000	38.9	703.3	742.2
2001	83.6	794.4	878.0
2002	57.5	595.1	652.6
2003	123.2	641.4	764.6
2004	107.9	603.3	711.2

Note: High yield bonds are below investment grade so likely to be more speculative and volatile.

Sources: Thomson Financial Securities Data; Bond Market Association

International bond and note issues

	2004, $bn	Outstanding, end Dec 2004
Floating rate issues	1,259	3,669
Straight fixed-rate issues	1,987	9,225
Equity-related issues	57	371
Money-market instruments	na	664
US dollar	1,155	na
Euro	1,598	na
Yen	112	na
Other currencies	439	na
Developed countries	3,012	12,475
United States	773	3,359
Euro area	1,463	6,209
Japan	62	298
Offshore centres	42	160
Emerging markets	152	737
Financial institutions	2,690	10,374
Private	2,276	8,747
Public	413	1,627
Corporate issuers	271	1,635
Private	231	1,361
Public	40	275
Governments	245	1,363
International organisations	97	556
Total announced issues, gross	3,303	13,928

Source: Bank for International Settlements

Bubbles that burst

Tulipmania

Tulips were introduced into western Europe from Turkey in the 16th century. In the 17th century they gave rise to one of the most curious episodes in Holland's history. In the early 1600s single-colour tulips were being sold at relatively modest prices in Dutch markets, but as new varieties were created the fashion for tulips intensified and prices soared. By 1623 a particularly admired and rare variety, *Semper Augustus*, was selling for 1,000 florins for a single bulb, more than six times the average annual wage. Ten years later the price had increased by more than fivefold, and then reached a peak at the height of the tulip craze of some 10,000 florins, roughly the same as it cost to buy a fine canalside house in the centre of Amsterdam.

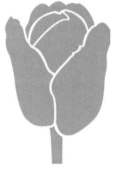

As the mania took hold more and more people sought to cash in on the boom, as the tulip business developed from dealing in actual bulbs to dealing in what were in effect tulip futures.

It couldn't last, and it didn't. In 1637 the bulb bubble burst when it became clear that at the end of the long chain of those speculating in bulb futures there was no one who actually wanted to buy the bulbs at such high prices. Within a period of a few months the market had crashed leaving thousands of people ruined.

The Mississippi Bubble

In 1716 John Law, a Scottish businessman who had come to France two years earlier, persuaded the French government, which was in financial distress, to let him set up a bank that could issue bank notes, which he believed would provide a spur to commerce and help get the government out of its financial difficulties. At the time France controlled the Louisiana colony, which covered an area larger than France itself. In August 1717 Law bought a controlling interest in the then derelict Mississippi Company and was granted a 25-year monopoly by the French government on trade with the West Indies and North America. The company acquired other French trading companies and was renamed the Compagnie des Indes, in effect controlling all French trade outside Europe. Law had raised money to fund the Mississippi Company's activities by issuing shares that could be purchased using notes issued by Law's Banque de Generale or government bonds.

As Law's business empire grew and there was more and more excitement about the riches that were to be exploited across the Atlantic, the share price rose dramatically. People from outside France as well as within couldn't get enough of the shares and Law issued more and more banknotes to enable people to buy them. By the end of 1819, the year of initial issue, the share price had increased twentyfold.

The crunch came at the beginning of 1820 when investors started to sell shares and realise their gains in gold. Law stepped in to prevent people being paid more than a certain amount in gold for their shares, with the rest being payable in notes. Within a year the share price had fallen to a tenth of its value at the peak and Banque de Generale notes were worth only half their face value. A year later the shares were back to their issue price, and Law subsequently took his leave of France. Opinion is divided as to whether Law was in fact a rogue or simply an honest man undone by a misguided scheme.

The South Sea Bubble

In 1711 the South Sea Company was given a monopoly of all trade to the South Seas in return for assuming a portion of the national debt that England had accumulated during the War of the Spanish Succession, which had started in 1703 and was still continuing. It was anticipated that when the war ended, which it did in 1713, there would be rich trade pickings to be had among the Spanish colonies in South America. But the South Sea Company did little trading, preferring to accumulate money from investors attracted by its future prospects.

War between Spain and England broke out again in 1718 and the following year the South Sea Company made a proposal to assume the whole of England's national debt. Inducements were offered to influential people and the proposal was accepted. New shares were issued in the company and the stock price was talked up and up.

Speculation fever took hold; a large number of companies that were to trade in the "New World" or which had other supposedly promising futures were set up, many of which were plain and simple scams to separate investors from their money. Confidence in the market was dented and in an effort encouraged by the managers of the South Sea Company to restore it, the "Bubble Act" was passed in 1720 requiring all joint stock companies to have a royal charter. It did the trick: the South Sea Company's share price increased more than fivefold in four months to reach over £1,000. And then the bubble burst – or rather started to deflate. A gradual slide in the share price accelerated and within three months the company was worthless. Many people were ruined and a committee set up in 1721 to investigate the affair discovered widespread corruption involving businessmen and politicians.

Railway mania

The British "railway mania" of the 1840s and the American railway boom up to 1873 shared many similarities. Rail

entrepreneurs used the stockmarket to raise huge sums to build proposed lines. Overinvestment led to excess capacity, failing revenues and defaults on loans – so much capital was diverted to railway projects that other businesses suffered and interest rates spiralled. In America, generous land grants helped railroad construction and around 170m acres was given to some 80 rail companies, though half the projected lines were never built. The railway bubble burst in the "Panic of 1873", the same year as America's first successful train robbery.

The Wall Street crash

In 1929 stock prices were 400% higher than they had been in 1924, pushed up way beyond any relationship with the actual worth of their companies, as investors, lured by the prospect of easy riches, piled into the market, accumulating some $6 billion of debt in the process. In early September 1929 prices fell sharply but recovered before falling again. In late October panic selling gave rise to the Wall Street crash, which ushered in a worldwide economic crisis, the Great Depression. Many shareholders were ruined, banks and businesses failed, and unemployment subsequently rose to around 17m.

Japan's monetary mistake

When through the Plaza Accord in 1985 Japan agreed to loosen its monetary policy to boost the value of the yen and trim its exports, things did not turn out quite as expected. Rather than restraining Japanese companies, the sudden doubling of the value of the yen against other currencies allowed big multinational firms to go on a buying spree of American and European assets, using bank loans and the rising value of their property portfolios as collateral. Bank lending on property ballooned as the initial loans drove up land prices and the higher land prices made those loans look like good business. At the height of the boom, the property around the imperial palace in Tokyo was worth more than California, and Australia paid off its national debt by selling a small parcel of land around its embassy. When the bubble burst after rises in interest rates in the early 1990s, property values slumped. Japan's banks and corporations have since struggled under the weight of bad debts and the country has endured years of economic stagnation that are partly attributable to the bubble and its bursting.

The dotcom boom and bust

The late 1990s saw a speculative frenzy of investment in internet-related shares as investors took the view that anything that would take advantage of the burgeoning popularity of the new technology was certain to make buckets of money. Venture capitalists threw money at any half-baked scheme as long as the entrepreneurs projected vast profits in a short space of time. Huge sums were spent on notional projects to build market share and vast increases in share price accompanied initial public offerings of the firms that were taken to market, making dotcom millionaires overnight (on paper at least). The dotcom boom rubbed off on other shares, especially technology stocks of any kind. Investors poured money into the stockmarket seeking to benefit from its seemingly inexorable rise.

In 1999 stockmarkets around the world hit record peaks. The January 2000 Super Bowl featured 17 dotcom companies which had each paid over $2m for a 30-second spot. But not long after, share prices for e-businesses started to fall as it finally struck home that firms were burning through cash with no prospect of ever making a profit. Eventually, all but the most robust dotcoms went to the wall, and stockmarkets plunged, with Nasdaq falling by over 70% between 1999 and 2002. In addition to the heavy losses incurred by institutional investors, millions of private investors lost substantial amounts of money, not to mention their confidence in the stockmarket.

Oil reserves and prices

Proven reserves, barrels, bn

	North America	South & Central America	Europe & Eurasia	Middle East	Africa	Asia Pacific
end 1984	101.9	36.3	96.7	430.8	57.8	38.1
end 1994	89.8	81.5	80.3	661.7	65.0	39.2
end 2004	61.0	101.2	139.2	733.9	112.2	41.1

Source: BP

Average oil price*

	$ per barrel		$ per barrel
1946	1.4	1987	19.2
1950	2.6	1988	16.0
1960	3.0	1989	19.6
1970	3.4	1990	24.5
1971	3.6	1991	21.6
1972	3.6	1992	20.6
1973	3.9	1993	18.4
1974	10.4	1994	17.2
1975	11.2	1995	18.4
1976	12.6	1996	22.0
1977	14.3	1997	20.6
1978	14.9	1998	14.4
1979	22.4	1999	19.3
1980	37.4	2000	30.3
1981	36.7	2001	25.9
1982	33.6	2002	26.1
1983	30.4	2003	31.0
1984	29.4	2004	41.4
1985	28.0	2005†	52.0
1986	15.1		

* West Texas Intermediate (WTI).

†Jan–Jan ave.

Sources: Dow Jones Energy Service; Thomson Datastream

Gold reserves and prices

Gold reserves and prices

	m ounces, year-end	Gold bullion av. price per troy oz, $
1970	1,059.74	35.65
1971	1,030.28	39.20
1972	1,021.52	49.30
1973	1,024.09	90.70
1974	1,022.08	174.70
1975	1,019.87	165.50
1976	1,015.38	128.70
1977	1,030.35	146.63
1978	1,037.98	170.63
1979	946.89	244.88
1980	955.52	525.50
1981	955.15	482.50
1982	951.23	352.00
1983	950.11	429.00
1984	948.98	378.00
1985	951.45	323.25
1986	951.44	344.75
1987	954.94	449.50
1988	946.65	451.50
1989	940.93	378.25
1990	938.90	370.50
1991	937.80	353.85
1992	928.86	337.00
1993	919.72	351.65
1994	915.67	375.20
1995	907.21	388.60
1996	905.38	391.90
1997	888.56	340.15
1998	968.41	308.05
1999	967.07	283.25
2000	952.09	275.25
2001	942.76	264.55
2002	930.55	308.00
2003	913.09	331.60
2004	900.22	391.75

Note: It was in 1971 that the dollar was finally cut loose from the gold standard, signalling the end of the Bretton Woods arrangements.

Sources: IMF: International Financial Statistics; Thomson Datastream

Gold facts

Gold is a yellow metal. Its chemical symbol is Au from the Latin word *aurum*, which means "glowing dawn".

Gold's atomic number is 79. Its specific gravity, a measure of density, is 19.3-times that of water and it is rated at about 2.5 on Moh's scale of hardness, placing it between gypsum and calcite.

Gold's proportion in an alloy is measured in karats. Pure gold is 24 karats, or 99.999% pure. 100% pure gold is almost impossible to refine. The word karat (and carat, the unit of weight used to measure gems) derives from the Italian *carato*, the Arab *qirat* or the Greek *keration*, all meaning the fruit of the carob or locust bean tree because the seeds of the fruit were once used to weigh gems and gold in oriental bazaars.

Gold is the most non-reactive of all metals. It does not react with oxygen and does not rust or tarnish.

Gold will only dissolve in acids such as aqua regia (a mixture of hydrochloric and nitric acids) and some others.

Gold is among the most electrically conductive of all metals. It can convey a tiny electrical current in temperatures between –55°C and 200°C.

Gold is the most ductile of all metals, allowing it to be drawn out into tiny wires or threads without breaking. A single ounce of gold can be drawn into a wire 5 miles long.

Gold's malleability is also unequalled. It can be shaped or extended into very thin sheets. One ounce of gold can be hammered into a 100-sq ft (9.3 sq m) sheet.

Total world production of gold down the ages is estimated at 3 billion ounces (85,000 tonnes). This would fit into a cube with sides measuring 55 feet (16.8m).

The world's most valuable gold coin is the 1933 American double eagle. In all, 445,500 coins were minted but were never circulated. All were melted down except one, which eventually fetched $7.6m at auction in 2002.

Source: The Gold Institute

Rich producers

Silver producers, 2003, tonnes

Peru	2,921
Mexico	2,551
China	2,000
Australia	1,868
Chile	1,313
Canada	1,309
Poland	1,237
US	1,236

Gold producers, 2003, tonnes

South Africa	373.3
Australia	282.0
US	276.1
China	194.4
Russia	176.9
Peru	173.0
Indonesia	164.4
Canada	141.5

Platinum producers, 2003, tonnes

South Africa	144.0
Russia	32.7
North America	9.2

Palladium producers, 2003, tonnes

Russia	91.8
South Africa	72.2
North America	29.4

Diamond producers, 2003

	Carats, million	$ million
Australia	31.0	400
Botswana	30.4	2300
Congo	25.0	400
Russia	19.0	1640
South Africa	12.8	950
Canada	11.2	1300
Angola	5.5	900
Namibia	1.5	450

Sources: World Bureau of Metal Statistics; Johnson Matthey; Mining Review

Diamond **and** platinum **facts**

Diamonds

Unlike precious metals, top diamond producers by volume are not the same countries as top diamond producers by value. Size and quality vary greatly. One carat = 0.2 grams.

The largest cut diamond is the Golden Jubilee, a yellow diamond weighing 545 carats now part of Thailand's crown jewels. The largest rough diamond is the Cullinan, weighing 3,107 carats and cut into two polished stones, the Great Star of Africa at 530 carats (the second largest polished diamond, now in the Tower of London) and the Lesser Star of Africa at 317 carats, and a further 104 stones.

The highest price paid at auction is the Star of the Season bought in 1995 for $16.5m. It is 100 carats. The diamond bought by Richard Burton for Elizabeth Taylor was 69 carats.

In 2003 thieves broke into the Diamond Centre in Antwerp and stole $100m worth of diamonds from safe-deposit boxes belonging to dealers and cutters.

A diamond was found in 2004 floating in space, the core of a dead star, weighing 10 billion trillion trillion carats, 2,500 miles across, bigger than the moon. It is 50 light years away.

Platinum

Platinum is generally 95% pure so does not tarnish or fade, and it is hypoallergenic. As well as being used for jewellery it has industrial and medical uses – catalytic converters and pacemakers.

Foreign-exchange trading

Daily turnover in traditional foreign-exchange markets averaged $1.9 trillion in the April 2004 triennial survey by the Bank for International Settlements, 36% more at constant exchange rates than in April 2001, reversing the fall between 1998 and 2001.

	Global turnover, % of total	
UK	31	
US	19	
Japan	8	
Singapore	5	
Germany	5	
Hong Kong	4	
Australia	3	
Switzerland	3	
France	3	
Canada	2	
Netherlands	2	
Other	15	

The dollar dominates trading, being on one side of 89% of all transactions. The euro represented 37%, yen 20%, sterling 16% and the Swiss franc 6%.

Global daily turnover in foreign exchange and interest-rate derivatives rose by 74% between 2001 and 2004 to $2.4 trillion a day. The global derivatives market reached a notional principal value of $220 trillion in June 2004.

Source: Bank for International Settlements

Venture capital

America

In 2003, the size of the average venture fund size in America was $145m, and there were approximately 700 venture-capital firms managing around $252 billion. In that year they invested about $18 billion in 2,227 companies, continuing the investment decline since the peak in 2000, when over $100 billion was invested in more than 5,000 companies.

Europe

In 2004, about €9 billion in venture-capital funds were raised throughout Europe and over €10 billion was allocated to 8,044 venture-capital investments, well below the peak in 2000 of just under €20 billion. Between 1980 and the end of 2004, European venture capital has earned an average annual return of 6% on investment.

Britain

Britain accounts for some 40% of the total European venture-capital market and is the second largest market after America. British venture-capital and private-equity funds have invested over £60 billion (£40 billion inside Britain) in more than 25,000 companies since 1983. London and the south-east of England received 47% of the British total in 2003, compared with 61% in 2002.

Stages of venture-capital financing

Seed finance: finance provided to research, assess and develop an initial concept before a business has reached the start-up phase.

Start-up: finance provided to companies for product development and initial marketing. Companies may be in the process of being set up or may have been in business for a short time, but have not sold their product commercially.

Other early stage: financing to companies that have completed the product development stage and require further funds to initiate commercial manufacturing and sales. They will not yet be generating a profit.

Expansion (or development): finance provided for the growth and expansion of a company which is breaking even or trading profitably. Capital may be used to finance increased production capacity, market or product development and/or to provide additional working capital.

Mezzanine (bridge finance): finance made available to a company in the period of transition from being privately owned to being publicly quoted.

Management buy-out: finance provided to enable current operating management and investors to acquire an existing product line or business.

Management buy-in: finance provided to enable a manager or group of managers from outside the company to buy into the company with the support of venture capital investors.

Sources: National Venture Capital Association; European Private Equity & Venture Capital Association; British Venture Capital Association; Department of Trade and Industry, Manufacturing Advisory Service

Hedge fund$

Hedge funds

Funds and dollars under management, 1999–2004, estimates

US hedge funds

	1999	2000	2001	2002	2003	2004
No. of funds	4,150	4,250	4,400	4,600	4,875	5,000
Amount under management , $bn	255	280	315	340	420	480

Offshore hedge funds

	1999	2000	2001	2002	2003	2004
No. of funds	2,050	2,250	2,600	2,900	3,225	3,700
Amount under management, $bn	225	240	285	310	400	470

Global hedge funds

	1999	2000	2001	2002	2003	2004
No. of funds	6,200	6,500	7,000	7,500	8,100	8,700
Amount under management, $bn	480	520	600	650	820	950

Source: Van Hedge Fund Advisors International

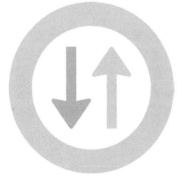

Investment [formulas]/²

Black-Scholes model

A pricing model for options that ranks among the most influential. It was devised by Fischer Black and Myron Scholes, two Chicago academics, in 1973, the year that formalised options trading began on the Chicago Board of Trade. Behind the model is the assumption that asset prices must adjust to prevent arbitrage between various combinations of options and cash on the one hand and the actual asset on the other.

Call price = $S [N(d_1)] - E/e^{rt}[N(d_2)]$

Where:
S = current stock price
$N(d_1)$ = normal distribution function of d_1
E = exercise price of option
e = the base of natural logarithms (= 2.718)
r = risk-free interest at an annual rate
t = time to expiry of option (as a fraction of a year)
$N(d_2)$ = normal distribution function of d_2

To solve for d_1:
$d_1 = [\ln(S/E) + (r + 0.5sd^2)t] / [sd(t)^{1/2}]$
Where:
$\ln(S/E)$ = the natural log of S/E
sd = the standard deviation of annual returns on the share price (where the share price is squared, it is the variance)

To solve for d_2:
$d_2 = d_1 - [sd(t)^{1/2}]$

Capital asset pricing model

Because of its comparative simplicity, the capital asset pricing model (CAP-M) is a much-used formula for modelling the theoretically correct price of assets and portfolios.

$E(R_s) = RF + \beta_s[E(R_m) - RF]$

Where:
$E(R_s)$ = the expected return on security $_s$
RF = the risk-free rate of return
β_s = the beta of security $_s$
$E(R_m)$ = the expected return on the market

Capital fulcrum point

An important formula for valuing a warrant, which measures the minimum annual percentage increase required from the value of the underlying ordinary shares for investors to hold warrants in a company's shares in preference to the shares themselves.

$$CFP = [(e/(s - w))^{1/y}] \times 100\%$$

Where:
e = exercise price
s = share price
w = warrant price
y = years to expiry of warrant

Capital market line

The graphical depiction of the trade-off between risk and return for an efficient portfolio. In other words, it is a chart line which shows how much extra return investors would expect for taking on extra risk.

$$[E(R_m) - RF]/[sd(R_m)]$$

defines the slope of the market line, where:
$E(R_m)$ = the expected return from the market
RF = the risk-free rate of return
$sd(R_m)$ = the standard deviation of returns from the market

Thus the expected return from any portfolio on the capital market line is:

$$E(R_p) = RF + \{[E(R_m) - RF]/[sd(R_m)]\}sd(R_p)$$

Where:
$E(R_p)$ = the expected return on portfolio $_p$
$sd(R_p)$ = the standard deviation of returns on portfolio $_p$

Dividend discount model

A tool for valuing a stock or share which says that the value of the share equals the present value of all its future dividends. It provides a basis for comparing the price of shares in the market with their theoretical value and thus judging whether the shares are cheap or expensive.

Where the growth rate in dividends is assumed to be constant, the fair price of a common stock can be stated as follows:

$P = D/(k - g)$

Where:
P = the price of the stock
D = expected dividend
k = the required rate of return
g = the expected growth rate in dividends

From this, the required rate of return can stated as:
$k = (D/P) + g$

and the stock's price/earnings ratio as:

$P/E = (D/E) / (k - g)$

Where:
E = the expected level of earnings

Single index model

Shows a security's return as a function of the market's return.

$R_{st} = a_s + b_s(R_{mt}) + e_{st}$

Where:
R_{st} = the return on security $_s$ over period $_t$
a_s = the constant return on security $_s$
b_s = the sensitivity of the security's return to the market's return (ie, its beta)
R_{mt} = the market's return over period $_t$
e_{st} = the difference between the actual return on $_s$ during a given period and its expected return

Source: *Essential Investment*, Philip Ryland, The Economist/Profile Books

Behind the currency name

Baht Until the 1940s the Thai currency was known as the tical. A *baht* was a unit of weight of around 15g, the equivalent in silver of one tical.

Bolivar Venezuela's currency takes its name from Simon Bolivar, a Venezulean known as "El Libertador" who led the defeat of Spanish colonialism in the 19th century, gaining independence for his own country as well as Bolivia, Colombia, Ecuador, Panama and Peru. Ecuador's sucre is named after Antonio José de Sucre, also an independence leader and one of Bolivar's closest friends.

Crown The French gold *"denier à la couronne"* was issued by Philip of Valois in about 1339 and featured a large embossed crown. The name was adopted by a slew of countries including the Czech Republic (koruna), Denmark (krone), Estonia (kroon), Iceland (króna), Norway (krone), Sweden (krona).

Dinar Its origin dates back to the most widely used Roman coin, the denarius. The silver coin's name means "containing ten" as it originally equalled ten copper *as*. It survives as the denar in Macedonia and dinar in Algeria, Bahrain, Iraq, Jordan, Kuwait, Tunisia and Serbia

Dollar The name is derived from that of the historic currencies of  Bohemia, the tolar, and Germany's thaler. The name *thaler* (from the German *thal*, meaning "valley") itself derives from the *guldengroschen* or "great gulden", a silver coin equal in value to a gold gulden and minted from the silver mined at Joachimsthal in Bohemia. The word "dollar" was in use in English for the thaler for about 200 years before America adopted the term. Spanish dollars, or "pieces of eight", were in circulation in Spain's colonies in the Americas in the 18th century. This and the Maria Theresa Thaler were both in wide use before the American revolution and lent their name to the country's new currency.

Drachma The Greek currency (now superseded by the euro) took its name currency from the verb "to grasp." The Arabic dirham's name is also derived from the ancient drachma.

Dram The Armenian word for "money".

Escudo Taken from the Portuguese (and Spanish) for "shield" and originally Spanish coins decorated with the coat of arms of the king of Spain – the great shield of the house of Hapsburg. The doubloon was a coin originally worth two escudos.

Franc The name is said to derive from the Latin inscription *francorum rex* ("King of the Franks") inscribed on gold coins first made during the reign of Jean le Bon (1350–64).

Guilder The name is taken from coins struck in Florence in the 13th century decorated with a lily, the *florensus,* derived from *fiorino,* Old Italian for flower. The Netherlands adopted the name *gulden,* short for *gulden florijn* (or golden florenus), of which guilder is a corruption. The abbreviation fl or f remained in use. The currency survives in Aruba and the Netherlands Antilles.

Kina Papua New Guinea's money takes its name from the kina shell, which was traditionally used as currency on the island.

Kuna The word means "marten" in Croatian, and is etymologically unrelated to the various currency names derived from the crown. It comes from the use of marten pelts as a trading commodity by medieval merchants.

Kwacha Zambia's currency is taken from the county's main language, Bemba. It means "dawn" and is taken from the country's nationalist slogan "new dawn of freedom".

Kwanza The official currency of Angola is named either after the Kwanza River or the Bantu word for "first".

Leu Dutch thalers circulating in Romania and Moldova in the 17th century bearing the impression of a lion were widely known as *lei* (lions). A form of the name was kept as a generic term for money (though becoming the lev in Bulgaria).

Lira The Vatican City and Malta retain a currency with a name originating from the value of a troy pound (Latin *libra*) of high purity silver. Turkey's lira shares the same root.

Manat In Azerbaijan and Turkmenistan the currency derives its name from Manah, a goddess of fate and destiny in pre-Islamic Arabia.

Mark An archaic unit of weight for precious metal in Europe equal to eight troy ounces, Germany's mark has been replaced by the euro but Bosnia has its marka and Finland its markka.

Pataca Macau's currency takes its name from a silver coin once popular in Asia, the Mexican eight *reales* or "pieces of eight", known in Portuguese as the Pataca Mexicana.

Peseta Spain's former currency takes its name from the Catalan word *peceta*, meaning "little piece".

Peso The Spanish word for "weight". The main colonial-era coin was worth eight *reales* (the "piece of eight") and was later called the *peso in* Argentina, Chile, Colombia, Cuba, Dominican Republic, Mexico, the Philippines and Uruguay.

Pound The term originates from the value of a troy pound weight of high purity silver. The symbol is based on a traditional capital "L" with a horizontal line through it, derived from the Latin word *libra*, meaning pound. Sterling dates back to the reign of Henry II in the 12th century and is probably derived from Easterling silver, mined in the area of Germany of the same name. It was famed for the high quality of its silver, which was imported to Britain to form the basis of coinage at the time. Another explanation is that sterling silver's hallmark featured a starling.

Pula In the Setswana language pula means "rain", a scarce and valuable resource in Botswana.

Quetzal Named after the national bird of Guatemala.

Rand South Africa's rand is named after gold-mining area in Transvaal, short for Witwatersrand

Real Brazil's money takes its name from the Portuguese and means "Royal currency". The basic silver unit of Spanish America was the real until about 1860.

Ringgit Malaysia's currency means "jagged" in Malay in reference to the serrated edges of Spanish silver dollars that circulated in the area.

Rouble The name is derived from the Russian word meaning "to chop". Historically, a ruble was a piece of silver chopped off an ingot.

Rupee India's currency takes its name from a Sanskrit word, *rupyah*, meaning "wrought silver".

Yen See Yuan.

Yuan China's currency is taken from the word meaning "round object" in Chinese. Japan's yen is taken from the same source.

Zloty Poland's currency means "golden" in Polish.

The oldest coins and notes

Lydia and the West

The first coins were made in the kingdom of Lydia in western Asia Minor (Turkey) in the 7th century BC. The Lydians grew wealthy from the alluvial gold they collected in the form of a gold-silver alloy called electrum and from the peoples and cities they ruled, including the Greek communities of the coast. These early coins were simply small, weighed nuggets of metal of variable shape, stamped on either side with an animal symbol and an abstract punch mark.

The earliest coin hoard consisting of electrum coins was found beneath the Temple of Artemis in Ephesus, one of the seven wonders of the Ancient World. It was discovered in 1904–05 during excavations undertaken by the British Museum. It was presumably placed in the foundations of the temple as a votive offering to the goddess.

In the mid-6th century the kingdom was ruled by King Croesus, made famous as the wealthiest man of his time by Herodotus, a Greek historian. During his reign the Lydians began to make pure gold and silver coins. He was overthrown by the Persians in 547 BC.

The Chinese tradition

At almost the same time coins began to be made in the various kingdoms of ancient China. They were cast bronze rather than struck precious metal and were anything but round. The earliest coins, in the shape of knives and small spades, were made in the Zhou kingdom in the late 7th or early 6th century BC.

Within three centuries all the other Chinese kingdoms had started to make coins. Spade-shaped coins were the most popular, but there were a number of different forms. The Chu kingdom's coins were bronze cowrie shells; the Qi state's coins resembled knives; and the coins of the Wei kingdom were round with a hole in the centre. These provided the model for traditional Chinese coinage until the end of the 19th century.

Banknotes in China and the East

The earliest forms of paper money were authorised in Song dynasty China (960–1279). They were produced to facilitate inter-regional trade in a period of increasing prosperity and expanding commerce within a huge country which otherwise used only low-value bronze or iron coins. At first they were exchange, remittance or credit notes with a date limitation.

In 1189, under the Jin dynasty (1115–1234), exchange certificates with no date limitation were issued. This was the first real paper money in free circulation. The Mongol Yuan dynasty (1206–1367) forbade the use of coins and allowed only paper money to circulate. Marco Polo commented on the strange custom of the use of paper for money in late 13th century China:

> *When these papers have been so long in circulation that they are growing torn and frayed, they are brought to the mint and changed for new and fresh ones at a discount of 3%. If a man wants to buy gold or silver ... he goes to the Khan's mint with some of these papers and gives them in payment ... All the Khan's armies are paid with this sort of money.*

The earliest banknotes in Europe

Sweden issued the earliest paper money in Europe. In 1656 a Livonian, Johan Palmstruch, founded the Stockholm Banco as a private institution with responsibility for managing the state's financial affairs. Sweden was rich in copper resources. To maintain the price of copper in world markets it introduced a non-token copper coinage to replace silver. The massive copper plates which resulted from this policy were heavy and inconvenient, so in 1661 Palmstruch hit on the idea of issuing paper credit notes as an alternative currency. Within a few years, however, the bank had issued too many notes and found it could no longer redeem them. In 1667 Palmstruch was accused of mismanagement and condemned to death. The sentence was later commuted.

More money *superlatives*

The most valuable coins ...

The highest prices these days are generally paid by American
collectors, and often for US coins, the rarest of which can sell for
large sums. In 2002 a 1933 gold double eagle ($20) coin was
bought by a private collector for $7,590,000 making it the most
expensive coin ever sold. The gold double eagle was minted in
1933 but all the coins were recalled and melted down before they
were issued, apart from ten which had been stolen by the Mint's
chief cashier. These were illegal to own, and federal agents tracked
down and recovered nine of them. In a 1996 sting operation the
tenth was found, but a few years later permission was given by the
American government to allow this (and only this) 1933 double
eagle to be privately owned, hence
its exceptionally high price.

> a 1933 gold double eagle coin was bought for 7,590,000 making it the most expensive coin ever old

Another coin less than 100 years
old – a 1913 Liberty Head nickel,
of which only five are known to
survive – was sold in June 2005 for
$4,150,000. Seven years earlier
this same coin had been the first to break the million-dollar price
barrier for a rare coin, when it sold in 1996 for $1,485,000.

A Roman gold coin of the usurper emperor Saturninus sold in
London for £264,000 in 1996, and six years earlier a unique gold
coin made by Brutus, the murderer of Julius Caesar in 44BC, sold
for $550,000. However, in 1980, a silver decadrachm of the city
of Acragas in Sicily made $572,000. Taking inflation into account,
this is the highest price ever realised for an ancient coin. The most
valuable medieval coins are sold for similar prices: in 2004 a
uniquely important British coin, a gold penny of Coenwulf (796-
821), sold for £230,000. Gold coins are always prized, and in June
2005 a 1643 gold Triple Unite of Charles I sold for $431,250. The
record price for an Islamic coin was realised in 1998, when a dinar
of al-Walid bin 'Abd al-Malik was sold for £308,000.

... and banknotes

Banknotes do not generally fetch such high prices, but six-figure
sums have been paid. Rarity, serial number and condition are

important in determining the value of a note. For example, a 1937–40 Mauritian 1,000 rupee note with the number A0000 sold at auction in London for £17,250, and a rare 1924 Australian £1,000 note sold in Melbourne for A$86,000. The auction record for an English banknote is £57,200, for a 1797 £1 note sold in 1993. As with coins, rare American banknotes are often more valuable because of the strength of the US market. In 1998 $126,000 was paid for a 1928 $10,000 Federal Reserve note, and in 2005 a $100 Treasury Note from 1890 sold for $356,500.

The biggest banknotes

Ever since their introduction banknotes have remained more or less the same size as they are now, with larger denominations tending to be somewhat bigger than smaller ones. However, in the 19th century notes were certainly larger than the current standard, sometimes up to twice the size. The largest banknotes ever to have been in general circulation are probably Chinese notes of the Ming dynasty: 1,000 cash notes made in the Hungwu reign (1368–98) measured 10 inches by 16 inches (26cm × 40cm). By contrast, the large "white fivers", the old British £5 notes sometimes seen in films of the 1940s and 1950s, which seem so large to modern-day viewers, measured only 8.25 by 5 inches (21cm × 13cm).

The highest denomination coins …

The earliest Lydian and Greek coins were of a high denomination, being made of electrum, a naturally occurring alloy of gold and silver, and large pieces of silver sometimes weighing up to 8 drachmas (32g). These coins were not intended for everyday use. The highest denomination coin (in real terms) ever made was probably the Mughal emperor Jahangir's 1,000 mohur gold coin (1613), a large gold presentation piece weighing almost 11kg.

In more recent times, an emergency issue of coins in the German state of Westphalia in 1923 included a coin with the value of 1 billion marks, and in 1946 Romania issued a silver coin with a face value of Lei100,000. Modern gold coins can often reach high denominational values. In 1970 Chad issued a Fr20,000 gold piece, and in the same year South Korea issued a W25,000 gold coin

a coin with the value of 1 billion marks

weighing almost 1kg. In 1975 Laos produced a K100,000 coin. In 1990 Greece issued a Dr20,000 coin to celebrate the 50th anniversary of the Italian invasion. These coins are not for everyday circulation and are often made in small quantities for collectors. Only 1,000 of the Greek coins were produced, for example. Of course, high denominations do not necessarily mean high values.

... and banknotes

In the modern world the effects of hyperinflation have produced some remarkably high denomination banknotes. In the early 1920s, Germany produced banknotes in increasingly large numbers and of ever higher values. In 1922 notes of thousands of marks became common, and in 1923 they passed 1m and reached 1 milliard (1,000m). In 1924 notes to the value of 1m million marks were produced. The record for the highest denomination banknote ever produced belongs to Hungary, which in 1946 made a note to the value of 100m billion peng. In Greece in 1944 bank-notes of Dr2,000m, Dr10,000m and Dr100,000m were produced.

More recently, the new states of eastern Europe and the Balkans have indulged in inflationary over-production of paper money. The paper currency of the breakaway Serb Republic in Bosnia quickly descended from sensible denominations of YuD10, YuD50 and YuD100 in 1992 to YuD50m, YuD100m and YuD500m in 1993. In Serbia itself in 1993 notes to the value of YuD500,000m were produced. A currency reform in 1994 rendered 1 new dinar equal to 1,000m old dinars.

The rarest old coins ...

Many issues of coin from the ancient world of Greece and Rome are rare, not necessarily because they were made in small quantities but simply because few have survived the accidents of history. Paradoxically, therefore, unique coins are not that unusual. One of the most important, now in the British Museum, is a coin of Octavian (later to become the emperor Augustus) of 28BC, the year when he claimed to be restoring the Roman Republic after 20 years of arbitrary rule and civil war, but was actually establishing himself as monarch. The inscription on the back reads, disingenuously, "He has restored to the People of Rome their laws and rights." Another unique coin of Augustus of 12BC shows the emperor raising a personification of the Roman Republic from her knees – the emperor as saviour of the state.

The usurper Roman emperor Silbannacus (mid-3rd century AD) is known to history solely because of the two surviving coins in his name. He is not mentioned in any ancient source. The existence of another rebel Roman emperor, Domitianus, who ruled Britain for a few days in 271AD, was confirmed in 2003 when a coin bearing his name was found in a hoard in Oxfordshire. One other coin in the name of Domitianus is known, but it was for years dismissed as a hoax.

In the modern world, among the most famous of rare coins is the 1933 British penny, of which only seven examples are known. In 1994 one was sold at auction for £20,000. News of this sale spread throughout the world, exciting the hopes of many who had pennies from 1932 or 1934, years when several million pennies were made.

❝ only seven examples of the 1933 penny are known ❞

But this cannot compare with the more than $4m paid in 2005 for one of the five known 1913 US Liberty Head nickels.

... and banknotes

Paper money, because of the material from which it is made, has less chance of surviving hundreds, let alone thousands, of years. However, paper money has often been mass-produced in huge quantities and certain notes of some historical periods, such as the American Civil War (1861–65), are still freely available. British banknotes from the 19th and early 20th centuries, particularly in high denominations (£200, £500, £1,000), are often rare and can fetch high prices at auction. The same is true for American high-denomination notes ($500, $1,000) of the same period. There is, for instance, only one known example of the 1891 $1,000 note, and all legal tender issues of 1869 are famously rare. From an earlier period, 14th-century Chinese paper money from the Ming dynasty (1368–1644) is, perhaps understandably given its age, also rare.

Notes and coins in circulation

US dollar

	Notes value, $bn	Coins value, $bn
1996	427.1	23.6
1997	458.0	24.3
1998	492.2	25.4
1999	601.2	27.2
2000	563.9	29.9
2001	612.3	31.1
2002	654.8	32.8
2003	690.2	33.9
2004	719.9	34.9

Pound

	Notes value, £bn	Notes quantity, bn
2001	27.2	0.98
2002	29.4	0.96
2003	33.9	1.03
2004	36.0	0.89

Euro

	Notes value, €bn	Notes quantity, bn
2002	115.0	4.78
2003	103.6	3.09
2004	108.0	1.58
2005	185.6	3.63

Sources: Financial Management Service, US Treasury; Bank of England; European Central Bank

Euros printed

Banknotes produced by Jan 1st 2002

	Quantity, m	Denomination	Quantity, m
Germany	4,342	5	2,415
France	2,570	10	3,013
Italy	2,380	20	3,608
Spain	1,924	50	3,674
Netherlands	655	100	1,246
Greece	581	200	229
Portugal	535	500	360
Belgium	530	Total	14,545
Austria	520		
Ireland	243		
Finland	219		
Luxembourg	46		
Total	14,545		

Source: European Central Bank

The life of $ and £ notes

$	Months, av.	£	Months, av.
1	21.3	5	12
5	24.4	10	36–48
10	25.0	20	36–48
20	21.8	50	60–120
50	55.4		
100	60.4		

Sources: Federal Reserve; Bank of England

Exchange rates

Period average	$1 = €	$1 = £	$1 = ¥
1950	na	0.36	361.10
1955	na	0.36	360.00
1960	0.63	0.36	360.00
1965	0.63	0.36	360.00
1970	0.66	0.42	360.00
1975	0.56	0.45	296.79
1980	0.65	0.43	226.74
1985	1.33	0.77	238.54
1990	0.77	0.56	144.79
1995	0.75	0.63	94.06
2000	1.09	0.66	107.77
2001	1.18	0.69	121.53
2002	1.06	0.67	125.39
2003	0.89	0.61	115.93
2004	0.81	0.55	108.19

Period average	$ = €1	$ = £1	$ = ¥1
1950	na	2.80	0.0028
1955	na	2.80	0.0028
1960	1.59	2.80	0.0028
1965	1.59	2.80	0.0028
1970	1.52	2.40	0.0028
1975	1.79	2.22	0.0034
1980	1.54	2.33	0.0044
1985	0.75	1.30	0.0042
1990	1.30	1.78	0.0069
1995	1.33	1.58	0.0106
2000	0.92	1.52	0.0093
2001	0.85	1.44	0.0082
2002	0.94	1.50	0.0080
2003	1.12	1.63	0.0086
2004	1.23	1.83	0.0092

Note: Synthetic $/€ rate until 1999.

Sources: IMF: International Financial Statistics; Thomson Datastream

Local currencies against the dollar

Local currencies against the dollar

	1980	end June 2005	% change
Japan	226.74	110.81	104.62
Switzerland	1.68	1.28	31.14
Singapore	2.14	1.69	26.83
United Arab Emirates	3.71	3.67	1.01
Qatar	3.66	3.64	0.59
Malta	0.35	0.35	-1.34
Canada	1.17	1.22	-4.47
Kuwait	0.27	0.29	-7.53
Denmark	5.64	6.16	-8.37
Oman	0.35	0.39	-9.09
Saudi Arabia	3.33	3.75	-11.20
UK	0.43	0.56	-22.93
Norway	4.94	6.54	-24.44
Cyprus	0.35	0.47	-26.10
New Zealand	1.03	1.44	-28.33
Australia	0.88	1.31	-32.92
Hong Kong	4.98	7.77	-35.93
South Korea	607.43	1,033.50	-41.23
Malaysia	2.18	3.80	-42.63
Sweden	4.23	7.81	-45.83
Thailand	20.48	41.32	-50.44
Morocco	3.94	9.06	-56.51
Jordan	0.30	0.71	-57.65
Tunisia	0.40	1.32	-69.73
Bangladesh	15.45	63.79	-75.78
Ethiopia	2.07	8.71	-76.23
China	1.50	8.28	-81.88
India	7.86	43.48	-81.92
Pakistan	9.90	59.61	-83.39
Sri Lanka	16.53	100.15	-83.49
Hungary	32.53	204.01	-84.06
Botswana	0.78	5.50	-85.82
Philippines	7.51	55.93	-86.57
Egypt	0.70	5.79	-87.92
Namibia	0.78	6.67	-88.31
South Africa	0.78	6.67	-88.31
Kenya	7.42	76.20	-90.26
Iceland	4.80	65.08	-92.62
Chile	39.00	579.15	-93.27
Indonesia	626.99	9,760.00	-93.58
Algeria	3.84	73.35	-94.76
Paraguay	126.00	6,060.00	-97.92
Colombia	47.28	2,325.50	-97.97
Iran	70.61	8,984.00	-99.21

Tanzania	8.20	1,127.00	-99.27
Malawi	0.81	122.99	-99.34
Nigeria	0.55	134.85	-99.59
Lebanon	3.44	1,506.50	-99.77
Israel	0.01	4.58	-99.78
Mexico	0.02	10.78	-99.81
Venezuela	4.29	2,633.81	-99.84
Mozambique	33.04	24,613.50	-99.87
Ecuador	25.00	25,000.00	-99.90
Romania	18.00	29,760.87	-99.94
Uruguay	0.01	24.64	-99.96
Ghana	2.75	9,089.00	-99.97
Sudan	0.05	247.02	-99.98
Zambia	0.79	4,665.00	-99.98
Zimbabwe	0.64	9,899.14	-99.99
Turkey	76.04	1,335,500.00	-99.99
Uganda	0.07	1,737.50	-100.00

Local currencies against the dollar

... and some younger currencies

	1994	end June 2005	% change
Lithuania	3.98	2.85	39.55
Czech Republic	28.79	24.83	15.95
Slovakia	32.04	31.68	1.15
Estonia	12.99	12.92	0.51
Croatia	6.00	6.04	-0.70
Latvia	0.56	0.58	-2.62
Macedonia	43.26	50.86	-14.94
Vietnam	10,965.67	15,851.00	-30.82
Poland	2.27	3.34	-32.05
Peru	2.19	3.25	-32.71
Slovenia	128.81	197.87	-34.90
Bolivia	4.62	8.09	-42.90
Argentina	1.00	2.89	-65.42
Brazil	0.64	2.36	-72.90
Russia	2.19	28.63	-92.35
Ukraine	0.33	5.01	-93.42
Suriname	0.13	2.74	-95.26
Bulgaria	0.05	1.62	-96.91

Euro

	Jan 4th 1999	end June 2005	% change
Euro area	0.85	0.83	2.69

Notes: As of 1 January 1st 2005 the currency of Turkey is the new Turkish lira equal to 1,000,000 old Turkish liras. As of July 1st 2005 the currency of Romania is the new Romanian leu equal to 10,000 old Romanian lei.

Exchange-rate pegs

Exchange rates can be tied to a particular currency as a currency union (eg, the countries in the euro area) or individually (eg, fixed to the US$). A peg reduces volatility, but it also reduces flexibility in monetary policy.

Euro currency members

Austria	Germany	Luxembourg
Belgium	Greece	Netherlands
Finland	Ireland	Portugal
France	Italy	Spain

Non-members pegged to the euro: Bosnia, Bulgaria, Cyprus, Denmark, Estonia, Hungary, Latvia, Lithuania, Malta, Slovenia

CFA franc zone, pegged to the euro

Benin	Congo-Brazzaville	Mali
Burkina Faso	Côte d'Ivoire	Niger
Cameroon	Equatorial Guinea	Senegal
Central African Rep.	Gabon	Togo
Chad	Guinea-Bissau	

Countries with currencies pegged to US$

Bahamas	Hong Kong	Oman
Bahrain	Jordan	Panama
Barbados	Kuwait	Qatar
Belize	Lebanon	Saudi Arabia
China	Malaysia	Seychelles
Ecuador	Maldives	Syria
El Salvador	Micronesia	United Arab Emirates
Eritrea	Netherlands Antilles	Venezuela

Eastern Caribbean Currency Union, pegged to the US$

Antigua and Barbuda	Grenada	St Lucia
Dominica	St Kitts and Nevis	St Vincent and the Grenadines

Source: IMF, as at December 2004

Some notable devaluations

Devaluations and revaluations are normally measured as changes in the value of one unit of national currency against the dollar; for example, Britain's devaluation in 1967 from $2.8 to $2.4 to the pound was 14.3%, and Argentina's devaluation in January 2002 from 1 peso to 1.4 pesos to the dollar was 28.6%.

Latin American currencies have had other big shifts, by devaluations or floating with or without official intervention.

Argentina has had many changes in the value and name of its currency (old peso, heavy peso, austral) until 1991's big bail-out brought in the new peso equal to the US dollar which lasted for 11 years.

In Mexico in1994 there was an official devaluation of 13%. But the peso continued to depreciate, and between the beginning of 1994 and the end of 1998 it had depreciated by 69%.

When Brazil's *real* floated in 1999 it depreciated by 23%.

South-east Asian currencies fell sharply during the 1997 financial crisis. During that year Indonesia's currency fell by 57%, South Korea's by 50% and Thailand's by 47%.

Russia's 1998 crisis caused the rouble to fall from 6.3 to the dollar in August to over 20 in December, a depreciation of almost 70%.

Turkey's currency went from 14 liras per dollar in 1975 to over 1,500,000 in 2004. On January 1st 2005 the new lira was introduced: 1 new lira = 1,000,000 old liras.

Market exchange rates, end 1995-end 2004, % falls

Turkish lira	95.5
Russian rouble	82.6
Indonesian rupiah	75.4
Argentinian peso	66.4
Brazilian real	63.4
Thai baht	35.2
Mexican peso	30.9
South Korean won	25.1

Sources: Press reports; IMF; Thomson Datastream

The changing world economy

Shares of world GDP at purchasing-power parity exchange rates, %

	1820	1870	1913	1950	1973	1998	2004*
Western Europe	23.6	33.6	33.5	26.3	25.7	20.6	19
US, Canada, Australia, New Zealand	1.9	10.2	21.7	30.6	25.3	25.1	24
Japan	3.0	2.3	2.6	3.0	7.7	7.7	7
China	32.9	17.2	8.9	4.5	4.6	11.5	13
Other Asia	23.3	18.8	13.0	11.0	11.8	18.0	20
Latin America	2.0	2.5	4.5	7.9	8.7	8.7	8
Eastern and Central Europe	8.8	11.7	13.1	13.1	12.9	5.3	6
Africa	4.5	3.7	2.7	3.6	3.3	3.1	3
World	100.0	100.0	100.0	100.0	100.0	100.0	100.0

* Estimated.
Sources: *The World Economy* by Angus Maddison; IMF

GDP per person, PPP$, 1990 prices

	1820	1870	1913	1950	1973	1998	2004*
US	1,257	2,445	5,301	9,561	16,689	27,331	34,500
Switzerland	1,280	2,202	4,266	9,064	18,204	21,367	25,400
Japan	669	737	1,387	1,926	11,439	20,413	25,100
France	1,230	1,876	3,485	5,270	13,123	19,558	24,500
Sweden	1,198	1,664	3,096	6,738	13,493	18,685	24,300
UK	1,707	3,191	4,921	6,907	12,022	18,714	24,100
Italy	1,117	1,499	2,564	3,502	10,643	17,759	21,700
Germany	1,058	1,821	3,648	3,881	11,966	17,799	21,400
Spain	1,063	1,376	2,255	2,397	8,739	14,227	18,500
Mexico	759	674	1,732	2,365	4,845	6,655	8,000
China	600	530	552	439	839	3,117	5,400
India	533	533	673	619	853	1,746	2,500
World	667	867	1,510	2,114	4,104	5,709	7,400

* Estimated.
Note: GDP is the sum of all output produced by economic activity. PPP statistics adjust for cost of living differences by replacing normal exchange rates with rates designed to equalise the prices of a standard "basket" of goods and services.
Sources: *The World Economy* by Angus Maddison; IMF; World Bank

Leading exporters

Biggest visible traders
% of world visible exports

Euro area	16.34	Russia	1.89
Germany	10.46	Switzerland	1.60
US	9.95	Malaysia	1.46
Japan	6.24	Sweden	1.42
China	6.09	Saudi Arabia	1.30
France	5.03	Austria	1.24
UK	4.28	Ireland	1.24
Italy	4.07	Singapore	1.11
Canada	3.97	Thailand	1.08
Netherlands	3.51	Brazil	1.02
Belgium	2.82	Australia	0.98
South Korea	2.75	Norway	0.96
Mexico	2.29	Denmark	0.90
Spain	2.22	Indonesia	0.88
Taiwan	1.99	Poland	0.85

Biggest invisible traders
% of world invisible exports

Euro area	19.25	China	1.92
US	18.30	Austria	1.81
UK	10.85	Sweden	1.64
Germany	7.14	Singapore	1.35
France	5.76	Denmark	1.31
Japan	5.28	South Korea	1.22
Italy	3.81	Taiwan	1.10
Netherlands	3.46	Norway	0.98
Spain	3.10	Australia	0.95
Switzerland	3.00	Russia	0.83
Canada	2.86	India	0.80
Hong Kong	2.74	Greece	0.80
Belgium	2.55	Turkey	0.65
Luxembourg	2.35	Thailand	0.58
Ireland	2.15	Finland	0.56

Sources: IMF, WTO and national statistics

Trade dependency

Average of exports plus imports

2003	% of GDP		% of GDP
Liberia	89.3	Panama	43.4
Malaysia	89.3	Latvia	43.1
Swaziland	83.9	Jordan	41.4
Singapore	78.4	Paraguay	41.1
Bahrain	76.6	Oman	40.9
Tajikistan	74.2	Trinidad & Tobago	40.3
United Arab Emirates	72.2	Mauritius	39.8
Slovakia	69.9	Costa Rica	38.4
Equatorial Guinea	66.5	Ghana	38.1
Belgium	65.7	Macedonia	37.9
Estonia	64.3	Tunisia	37.7
Belarus	61.2	Kazakhstan	37.6
Malta	59.8	Azerbaijan	37.5
Czech Republic	58.5	Nicaragua	37.4
Vietnam	57.5	Honduras	36.9
Moldova	56.9	Kuwait	36.7
Mongolia	54.8	Kirgizstan	36.4
Hungary	54.5	Croatia	36.2
Cambodia	54.0	Switzerland	36.2
Libya	52.5	Botswana	36.0
Turkmenistan	51.0	Austria	35.4
Qatar	50.8	Yemen	34.6
Thailand	50.6	Côte d'Ivoire	33.4
Slovenia	50.3	Romania	32.9
Eritrea	49.4	Armenia	32.7
Angola	49.0	Gabon	32.3
Bosnia	49.0	Namibia	32.1
Luxembourg	48.2	West Bank and Gaza	32.1
Ukraine	48.2	Canada	31.8
Suriname	47.9	Malawi	31.8
Ireland	47.6	Nigeria	31.0
Netherlands	46.7	South Korea	30.8
Lithuania	46.7	Sweden	30.8
Taiwan	45.8	Poland	30.5
Guinea-Bissau	44.3	Jamaica	30.2
Philippines	44.0	Sri Lanka	30.1
Bulgaria	43.7	El Salvador	29.9

2003	% of GDP		% of GDP
Saudi Arabia	29.6	Kenya	21.6
China	29.5	Chad	21.0
Uzbekistan	29.3	France	20.7
Georgia	29.2	Italy	19.6
Finland	28.6	Bahamas	19.5
Algeria	28.5	Uruguay	19.5
Senegal	28.4	UK	19.3
Zambia	28.4	Bolivia	19.1
Israel	28.3	Benin	18.6
Germany	28.2	Guatemala	18.6
Denmark	28.1	Cameroon	18.4
Congo-Brazzaville	27.2	Ethiopia	18.3
Chile	27.0	Albania	18.2
Mexico	26.8	Colombia	17.4
Portugal	26.4	Guinea	17.3
Serbia	26.2	Pakistan	17.3
Gambia, The	25.6	Tanzania	17.3
Barbados	25.3	Argentina	16.5
Norway	24.8	Niger	16.3
Indonesia	24.7	Bangladesh	15.7
Zimbabwe	24.7	Australia	15.1
Morocco	24.6	Greece	14.7
Russia	24.5	Uganda	14.6
Turkey	24.5	Sudan	14.3
Mozambique	24.4	Peru	14.1
Congo	24.0	Burkina Faso	14.0
Iceland	23.7	Hong Kong	13.8
Syria	23.7	Egypt	13.5
Ecuador	23.2	Burundi	12.5
South Africa	23.0	Brazil	12.3
Lebanon	22.9	India	10.6
Iran	22.6	Central African Rep	10.2
New Zealand	22.4	Japan	9.2
Venezuela	22.3	Rwanda	9.2
Cyprus	22.2	Cuba	9.1
Laos	22.2	US	9.1
Mali	22.1	Somalia	4.4
Spain	21.6	Myanmar	3.0

Sources: IMF, WTO, and national statistics.

Foreign direct investment

Inflows, $bn

	1992–97 ave.	1998	1999	2000	2001	2002	2003	Stocks, % of GDP, end 2003
EU	95.8	249.9	479.4	671.4	357.4	374.0	295.2	32.8
Other Western Europe	5.0	13.1	20.7	26.0	11.4	6.2	15.1	37.1
North America	68.3	197.2	308.1	380.8	186.9	83.9	36.4	15.4
Other developed countries	11.7	12.3	20.2	29.8	15.7	25.8	20.0	6.7
Africa	5.9	9.1	11.6	8.7	19.6	11.8	15.0	25.3
Latin America & the Caribbean	38.2	82.5	107.4	97.5	88.1	51.4	49.8	36.8
Other Asia	74.5	102.4	112.9	146.2	112.0	94.5	107.3	30.3
Central & eastern Europe	11.5	24.3	26.5	27.5	26.4	31.2	21.0	23.7
Total	310.9	690.8	1,086.8	1,387.9	817.5	678.8	559.8	22.9

Developing economies with the biggest inflows in 2003

	1992–97 ave.	1998	1999	2000	2001	2002	2003	Stocks, % of GDP, end 2003
China	32.8	45.5	40.3	40.7	46.9	52.7	53.5	35.6
Hong Kong	7.8	14.8	24.6	61.9	23.8	9.7	13.6	236.5
Singapore	8.3	7.7	16.1	17.2	15.0	5.7	11.4	161.3
Mexico	9.6	12.3	13.2	16.6	26.8	14.7	10.8	26.5
Brazil	6.6	28.9	28.6	32.8	22.5	16.6	10.1	25.8
Bermuda	2.4	5.4	9.5	10.6	13.3	2.7	8.5	3,052.0
Cayman Is.	0.9	4.4	6.6	6.9	4.4	2.5	4.6	3,157.0
India	1.7	2.6	2.2	2.3	3.4	3.4	4.3	5.4
South Korea	1.3	5.0	9.4	8.6	3.7	2.9	3.8	7.8

Note: Foreign direct investment (FDI) is long-term investment in companies in a foreign country, implying a certain degree of control of those companies. Stocks indicate the value of those investments.

Source: United Nations Conference on Trade and Development

Sending money home

Workers overseas send about $100 billion back to their home
country each year, and it is growing at double-digit rates. India
received over $17 billion from overseas in 2003, nearly double the
2000 amount. Mexico has more than doubled its inflow, to over
$13 billion. Other rapidly growing recipients are Pakistan (nearly
four times the 2000 amount), China (more than six times) and
Guatemala (nearly four times).

Countries' receipts, $bn	2000	2001	2002	2003
India	9.2	8.4	13.7	17.3
Mexico	6.6	8.9	9.8	13.4
Spain	3.4	3.7	4.0	4.7
Pakistan	1.1	1.5	3.6	4.0
Morocco	2.2	3.3	2.9	3.6
China	0.6	0.9	1.7	3.3
Bangladesh	2.0	2.1	2.8	3.2
Colombia	1.6	2.0	2.5	3.1
Egypt	2.9	2.9	2.9	3.0
Portugal	3.2	3.3	2.7	2.8
Serbia	1.1	1.7	2.1	2.7
Guatemala	0.6	0.6	1.6	2.1
El Salvador	1.8	1.9	1.9	2.1
Dominican Republic	1.7	1.8	2.0	2.1
Brazil	1.1	1.2	1.7	2.0

Source: World Bank

Interest rates

Short-term rates
London interbank offer rates, %

	US	UK	Japan	Euro area
1979	12.09	13.88	6.08	
1980	14.19	16.35	11.30	
1981	16.87	14.32	7.73	
1982	13.29	12.58	6.99	
1983	9.72	10.18	6.57	
1984	10.94	10.02	6.43	
1985	8.40	12.25	6.68	
1986	6.86	10.97	5.12	
1987	7.18	9.80	4.26	
1988	7.98	10.36	4.51	
1989	9.28	13.94	5.46	
1990	8.31	14.79	7.76	
1991	5.99	11.67	7.38	
1992	3.86	9.70	4.46	
1993	3.29	6.06	3.00	
1994	4.74	5.54	2.31	
1995	6.04	6.73	1.27	
1996	5.51	6.09	0.63	
1997	5.76	6.90	0.63	
1998	5.57	7.39	0.72	
1999	5.41	5.54	0.22	2.96
2000	6.53	6.19	0.28	4.41
2001	3.78	5.04	0.15	4.26
2002	1.80	4.06	0.08	3.32
2003	1.22	3.73	0.06	2.33
2004	1.62	4.64	0.05	2.11
2005 April	3.15	4.94	0.05	2.14

Source: Thomson Datastream

Some notable highs Money-market interest rates in Argentina averaged nearly 1.4m% in 1989 and over 9m% in 1990. Russian rates averaged 190% in 1995. Zimbabwe's rates averaged over 100% in 2003 and 2004. Turkey's interbank money-market rate came down from an average of 92% in 2001 to 16.9% in early 2005.

Central bank rates

America The US federal funds rate went from 4.75% in 1977 to 19% in 1981. Its next low point was 3% in 1993 before going up to 6.5% in 2000. The 45-year low point of 1% ran from June 2003 to June 2004, then rising in eight quarter-point moves to 3% by May 2005.

Britain The UK's minimum lending rate went to 15% in 1976, down to 5% in 1977 then up to 17% in 1979. MLR was replaced with the "Minimum Bank 1 Dealing Rate" in August 1981. This came down to below 8% in 1988. On Black Wednesday (September 16th 1992) the rate went briefly up to 15%. The repo rate, which became the new official rate in May 1997, went to a low of 3.5% in July 2003 then rose in five quarter-point stages to 4.75% in August 2004.

Japan The Bank of Japan's official discount rate was set at a high of 9% in 1973 and again in 1980. It has been 0.10% since September 2001. The target call rate minimum in May 2005 was 0.001%

Sources: IMF; Federal Reserve; Bank of England; Bank of Japan

Corporate tax rates

Average, %

	1998	2004	% change, 1998–2004
OECD	35.67	29.96	-16.01
EU	36.17	31.32	-13.41
Latin America	32.03	30.02	-6.28
Asia Pacific	29.96	30.37	1.37
Argentina	33.00	35.00	6.06
Australia	36.00	30.00	-16.67
Austria	34.00	34.00	0.00
Bangladesh	40.00	30.00	-25.00
Belgium	40.17	33.99	-15.38
Belize	35.00	25.00	-28.57
Bolivia	25.00	25.00	0.00
Brazil	25.00	34.00*	36.00
Canada	44.60	36.10	-19.06
Chile	15.00	17.00	13.33
China	33.00	33.00	0.00
Colombia	35.00	35.00	0.00
Costa Rica	30.00	30.00	0.00
Czech Republic	35.00	28.00	-20.00
Denmark	34.00	30.00	-11.76
Dominican Republic	25.00	25.00	0.00
Ecuador	36.25	36.25	0.00
El Salvador	25.00	25.00	0.00
Fiji	35.00	31.00	-11.43
Finland	28.00	29.00	3.57
France	41.66	34.33	-17.59
Germany†	50.13	38.29	-23.62
Greece†	37.50	30.00	-20.00
Guatemala	25.00	31.00	24.00
Honduras‡	35.00	25.00	-28.57
Hong Kong	16.50	17.50	6.06
Hungary	18.00	16.00	-11.11
Iceland**	33.00	18.00	-45.45
India	35.00	35.88	2.50
Indonesia	30.00	30.00	0.00
Ireland	32.00	12.50††	-60.94
Italy	41.25	37.25	-9.70
Japan	51.60	42.00	-18.60

	1998	2004	% change, 1998–2004
South Korea	30.80	29.70	-3.57
Luxembourg	37.45	30.38	-18.88
Malaysia	28.00	28.00	0.00
Mexico	34.00	33.00	-2.94
Netherlands	35.00	31.75	-9.29
New Zealand	33.00	33.00	0.00
Norway	28.00	28.00	0.00
Pakistan	30.00	35.00	16.67
Panama	37.00	30.00	-18.92
Papua New Guinea	25.00	30.00	20.00
Paraguay	30.00	30.00	0.00
Peru	30.00	30.00	0.00
Philippines	34.00	32.00	-5.88
Poland	36.00	19.00	-47.22
Portugal	37.40	27.50	-26.47
Russia	na	24.00	na
Singapore	26.00	22.00	-15.38
South Africa	na	37.80	na
Spain	35.00	35.00	0.00
Sri Lanka	35.00	35.00	0.00
Sweden	28.00	28.00	0.00
Switzerland	27.80	24.10	-13.31
Taiwan	na	25.00	na
Thailand	30.00	30.00	0.00
Turkey	44.00	33.00	-25.00
Ukraine	na	25.00	na
UK	31.00	30.00	-3.23
US	40.00	40.00	0.00
Uruguay	30.00	35.00	16.67
Venezuela	34.00	34.00	0.00
Vietnam†	32.50	28.00	-13.85

*Includes social contribution tax on profits.
†Average rate from a tax band.
‡Excludes high-income surcharges.
**Applies to limited liability companies only.
††Applies to active income only; 25% for passive income.
Source: KPMG

What companies pay in tax

Total, $bn

	1970	1980	1990	2000	2003
Australia	1.62	5.52	12.86	25.18	21.62*
Canada	3.04	10.04	14.73	32.08	32.13
Czech Republic	na	na	na	1.97	4.12
France	3.15	14.22	27.85	40.68	44.85
Germany	3.45	16.88	26.58	34.16	30.71
Hungary	na	na	na	1.04	1.54*
Ireland	0.11	0.30	0.79	3.58	5.82
Italy	1.84	10.65	43.00	31.57	41.66
Japan	10.83	60.07	202.29	173.70	133.55
South Korea	na	1.22	6.72	17.04	23.62
Spain	0.52	2.60	14.93	16.96	26.29
Sweden	0.59	1.50	4.00	9.68	7.73
Switzerland	0.37	1.81	4.69	6.77	8.51
Turkey	0.14	0.51	2.01	4.69	6.25
UK	3.98	15.76	35.43	52.14	50.01
US	36.57	78.62	140.61	254.98	215.89

Per head of population, $

	1970	1980	1990	2000	2003
Australia	126	373	749	1,307	1,095*
Canada	142	410	532	1,042	823*
Czech Republic	–	–	–	192	404
France	61	258	479	671	729
Germany	57	274	420	416	372
Hungary	–	–	–	102	151*
Ireland	36	88	224	942	1,157*
Italy	34	189	758	547	658*
Japan	104	514	1,637	1,369	977*
South Korea	–	32	157	363	493
Spain	15	69	384	425	644
Sweden	74	181	467	1,091	863
Switzerland	60	284	690	939	998*
Turkey	4	12	36	70	59*
UK	72	280	619	889	762*
US	178	345	562	903	742

*2002.

Source: OECD

What individuals pay in tax

Total, $bn

	1970	1980	1990	2000	2003
Australia	3.56	19.96	39.08	44.89	49.70*
Canada	8.73	29.46	85.47	96.73	101.51
Czech Republic	na	na	na	2.58	4.44
France	5.37	32.19	55.74	106.10	135.02
Germany	16.20	91.61	151.67	178.90	206.27
Hungary	na	na	na	3.38	5.04*
Ireland	0.22	2.09	5.06	9.12	11.97
Italy	3.05	31.52	112.57	115.62	158.07
Japan	8.84	66.94	251.36	266.09	191.06
South Korea	na	1.26	8.94	17.64	19.51
Spain	0.73	10.40	36.77	36.89	57.00
Sweden	6.67	25.15	49.19	42.28	47.97
Switzerland	1.64	11.14	23.81	26.17	32.55
Turkey	0.60	5.37	8.08	14.32	12.34
UK	14.44	55.47	105.92	158.26	182.24
US	101.27	285.51	582.82	1,223.59	976.45

Per head of population, $

	1970	1980	1990	2000	2003
Australia	277	1,348	2,275	2,329	2,516*
Canada	409	1,202	3,085	3,142	2,842*
Czech Republic	–	–	–	251	435
France	103	584	958	1,751	2,194
Germany	267	1,488	2,398	2,177	2,500
Hungary	–	–	–	331	497*
Ireland	75	616	1,442	2,401	2,311*
Italy	57	559	1,985	2,002	2,219*
Japan	85	573	2,035	2,097	1,478*
South Korea	–	33	209	375	407
Spain	21	277	947	924	1,397
Sweden	829	3,027	5,747	4,766	5,355
Switzerland	262	1,745	3,504	3,630	3,887*
Turkey	17	121	144	212	145*
UK	260	985	1,851	2,699	2,811*
US	494	1,254	2,330	4,332	3,355

*2002.
Source: OECD

How taxing for top earners?

Top personal income tax rate, %

	1975	1980	1985	1990	1995	2000	2004
Australia	65.0	60.0‡	60.0	48.0	47.0	47.0	48.5
Austria	62.0	62.0	62.0	50.0	50.0	50.0	42.9
Belgium	60.0	76.3	71.6	55.0	55.0	52.6	45.1
Canada	47.0	62.8‡	34.0	29.0	29.0	44.7	46.4
Denmark	40.0	70.0‡	39.6	68.0	63.5	54.3	54.9
France	60.0	60.0	65.0	51.8	56.8**	47.3	37.0
Germany	56.0	56.0	56.0	53.0	53.0	53.8	47.5
Greece	63.0	60.0	63.0	50.0	45.0	45.0	33.6
Ireland	77.0	60.0	65.0	56.0	48.0	44.0	42.0
Italy	72.0	72.0	65.0	50.0	51.0	46.4	41.4
Japan	75.0	75.0	70.0	50.0	50.0	45.5	47.1
Luxembourg	57.0	58.4	57.0	56.0	50.0	47.2	33.9
Mexico	42.0*	55.0	55.0	35.0	35.0	40.0	26.6
Netherlands	71.0	72.0	72.0	60.0	60.0	60.0	52.0
New Zealand	60.0	60.0	66.0	33.0	33.0	39.0	39.0
Portugal	91.0†	77.5‡	60.0	40.0	40.0	35.6	35.6
South Korea	63.0*	79.1‡	55.0	50.0	45.0	44.0	36.6
Spain	62.0	65.5	66.0	56.0	56.0	48.0	45.0
UK	83.0	60.0‡	60.0	40.0	40.0	40.0	40.0
US	70.0	70.0	50.0	28.0	39.6	46.7	41.4

*1974. †1976. ‡1981. **1994.

Note: Data for 2000 and 2004 are taken from the OECD tax database which combines the central and sub-central government tax rates. Data for previous years are taken from the World Tax Database (WTD), Office of Tax Policy Research. The rates may not necessarily agree between the OECD and WTD due to slight differences in the calculation of the tax rate.

Sources: OECD; World Tax Database, Office of Tax Policy Research

VAT and sales tax rates

2004	%		%
Denmark	25.0	Slovakia	19.0
Hungary	25.0	Estonia	18.0
Sweden	25.0	Greece	18.0
Norway	24.0	Latvia	18.0
Finland	22.0	Lithuania	18.0
Poland	22.0	Malta	18.0
Belgium	21.0	UK	17.5
Ireland	21.0	Germany	16.0
Austria	20.0	Spain	16.0
Italy	20.0	Canada*	15.0
Slovenia	20.0	Cyprus	15.0
France	19.6	Luxembourg	15.0
Czech Republic	19.0	Switzerland	7.6
Netherlands	19.0	US (lowest)†	2.9
Portugal	19.0	US (highest)†	7.0

*Harmonised sales tax (HST).
†Lowest: Colorado; highest: Mississippi, Rhode Island and Tennessee.
Sources: KPMG; The Tax Foundation

Wealth and debt

Net wealth as % of disposable income

	1993	2003*
Italy	782.4	810.9
Japan	772.3	753.1
UK	582.9	724.5
France	516.0	606.6
US	489.6	545.2
Canada	457.2	515.0
Germany	481.8	508.9

*2002 for Italy and Japan.

Note: Net wealth is total assets (non-financial and financial) minus liabilities (consumer debt). Non-financial assets include stock of durable goods and dwellings. Financial assets comprise currency & deposits, securities (except shares), loans, shares and other equity. Disposable income is after-tax income, available for spending or saving.

Consumer debt as % of disposable income

	1993	2003*
UK	106.5	138.9
Japan	132.1	135.8
Canada	99.5	119.8
US	89.7	118.1
Germany	91.0	111.6
France	82.6	78.6
Italy	31.8	39.3

*2002 for Italy and Japan.
Source: OECD

Offshore attractions

Offshore banks

2003	No.
Cayman Islands	580
Switzerland	500
Bahamas	301
Luxembourg	200
Guernsey	65
Isle of Man	57
Barbados	56
Vanuatu	55
Labuan (Malaysia)	54
Bahrain	52
Singapore	50
Netherlands Antilles	39
Panama	34

Source: US Department of State

Tax havens

Andorra*	Gibraltar	Nauru
Anguilla	Grenada	Marshall Islands*
Antigua & Barbuda	Guernsey	Samoa
Aruba	Isle of Man	San Marino
Bahamas	Jersey	Seychelles
Bahrain	Liberia*	St Christopher (St Kitts)
Barbados	Liechtenstein*	and Nevis
Belize	Malta	St Lucia
Bermuda	Mauritius	St Vincent and the
British Virgin Islands	Monaco*	Grenandines
Cayman Islands	Montserrat	Turks & Caicos
Cook Islands	Netherlands Antilles	US Virgin Islands
Cyprus	Niue	Vanuatu
Dominica	Panama	

*These countries have not committed to cooperating on effective information exchange and transparency with the OECD

Notes: A tax haven has three criteria according to the OECD – no or nominal taxes; lack of effective information exchange; inadequate transparency. All tax havens listed have agreed to address "harmful tax practices" by Dec 31st, 2005 with the OECD.

Source: OECD

Great business books

Here is a list of 20 business books that stand out from the crowd that have been published over the years.

Barbarians at the Gate
Bryan Burrough and John Helyar, 1990
The fall of RJR Nabisco

Built to Last
Jim Collins and Jerry Porras, 1994
What it takes to endure

Competitive Strategy
Michael Porter, 1980
How to gain competitive advantage

Corporate Strategy
Igor Ansoff, 1965
The ABC of strategic planning

The Dilbert Principle
Scott Adams, 1996
The foolish ways of managers

Future Shock
Alvin Tofler, 1970
Fast change is traumatic and inevitable

The Human Side of Enterprise
Douglas McGregor, 1960
The origin of Theories X and Y

In Search of Excellence
Tom Peters and Robert Waterman, 1982
Boosting the ego of corporate America

Liar's Poker
Michael Lewis, 1990
Wall Street laid bare

The Machine that Changed the World
James Womack, Dan Jones and Daniel Roos, 1991
The story of lean production

Microserfs
Douglas Coupland, 1995
Get a life in Silicon Valley

My Years with General Motors
Alfred Sloan, 1963
How GM was built – by the man who did it

The One Minute Manager
Kenneth Blanchard and Spencer Johnson, 1981
Keep it simple … and swift

The Peter Principle
L.J. Peter and R. Hull, 1969
The rise of the incompetent

The Principles of Scientific Management
Frederick Winslow Taylor, 1911
The very first business bestseller

Re-engineering the Corporation
Michael Hammer and James Champy, 1993
Revolution through process design

Small is Beautiful
E.F. Schumacher, 1973
The title says it all

The Smartest Guys in the Room
Bethany McLean and Peter Elkind, 2003
The best telling of the scandalous fall of Enron

Strategy and Structure
Alfred Chandler, 1962
Why structure follows strategy

Up the Organisation
Robert Townsend, 1970
Ex-Avis boss teaches the
world how to try harder

Compiled by Tim Hindle

What's in a word?

Many terms and expressions are used in business without people giving a second thought to how they have come about. Here are the origins of some popular ones.

Bear A speculator who sells securities in the expectation that prices will fall. Bears may sell short, ie, sell securities they do not own, leading to suggestions that the expression refers to the phrase "selling the skin before you have caught the bear". Trappers were also in the habit of short selling their wares. Short sellers were called "bearskin jobbers" in 18th century London.

Bellwether The term for a closely watched company that indicates the fortunes of an entire industry takes its name from castrated male sheep that lead flocks. These sheep used to wear bells to help shepherds find them in the dark or in bad weather.

Benchmark The technique for comparing performance in business and finance refers to a surveyor's mark made on a stationary object for use as a reference point for subsequent observations.

Big cheese Important people may have derived their epithet from colonial India. The Urdu word *"chiz"*, which means thing, like so many other phrases was taken up by the British. Its meaning was altered to mean "good".

Blue chip An American term referring to the colour of the highest value poker chip.

Boss The Dutch word *"baas"*, meaning master, was adopted in America from Dutch colonisers and in South Africa by the British from the Afrikaners.

The buck stops here American poker players in the 19th century would use a bit of buckshot to denote which player was the dealer and so had ultimate responsibility to pass out the cards.

Bull An investor who buys in the hope that prices will rise. Probably named just to contrast them with bears. Bull and bear baiting were popular sports in Britain at the time that the forerunner of the modern stockmarket first emerged.

Cash cow Came into common usage only recently but the term milch cow was used as early as the 17th century to mean a dependable source of prosperity.

Dead cat bounce A small improvement in a bear market is so called because "even dead cats bounce".

Dead wood Someone or something serving no purpose, taken from a technique in shipbuilding. Timbers were laid on the keel for no other reason that to make it a little more rigid.

Line your pockets It has been suggested that the term originates from the practice of tailors in Regency England to send garments to George "Beau" Brummell stuffed with banknotes in order to seek the patronage of the famous dandy and fashion leader.

Pac-Man strategy A measure to avoid takeover whereby the intended target counterattacks by making an offer for the firm that is trying to acquire it, named after the 1980s arcade game.

Pay through the nose The Danes of the 9th century imposed a "nose" tax on the Irish, so-called because those who avoided paying had their nostrils slit.

Poison pill An anti-takeover measure that attempts to make the potential acquiree a less attractive target, named after the cyanide pills that enemy agents swallow in the event of capture.

Red tape British lawyers and government officials formerly used to bind documents together with red cloth tape. The term was first used to describe bureaucracy by Charles Dickens.

Tycoon Wealthy and successful businessmen get their names from the Japanese "*taikun*", a powerful military leader. The word became popular in the early part of the 20th century.

Stag Someone who applies for an allotment of shares in an initial public offering, with a view to selling them straight away at a healthy premium. It is suggested that the term originates because stag is also a term used for a castrated bull.

White knight A friendly potential buyer of a firm that is threatened by a less welcome suitor. In *Alice through the Looking Glass* the heroine is captured by the red knight but is rescued at once by the white knight.

LATIN **that lawyers like to use**

A fortiori	for a compelling reason
Ad valorem	value
Affidavit	he has said it (a sworn statement)
Bona fide	in good faith, honestly, sincerely, without deception (**Mala fide** in bad faith)
Bona vacantia	vacant goods; goods without an owner
Caveat emptor	buyer beware
De minimis non curat lex	the law is not concerned with trivial matters
De facto	in point of fact
Eiusdem generis	of the same kind
Ex gratia	as a favour; without liability
Ex parte	on behalf of one party
Fieri facias	make it happen
Functus officio	having shot one's bolt; spent
Habeas corpus	let him have his body back
Habendum	the part of a conveyance of real estate that describes how the property is to be transferred to the transferee
Ignorantia legis non excusat	ignorance of the law is not an excuse
In flagrante delicto	in the act of committing a crime
In personam	in respect of the person; personally
In re	in the matter of
In rem	in respect of the thing; reality
Inter alia	among other things
Inter partes	between the parties
Inter vivos	between living people
Intra vires	within the permitted powers
Ipso facto	by the very fact itself
Lex fori	the law of the place where the case is being heard
Lex loci	the law of the place where the act was done
Locus standi	official standing; recognition
Mala in se	wrongs in themselves
Mala prohibita	forbidden wrongs

Mandamus	we command
Mens rea	guilty mind
Mens sana in sano corpore	a sound mind in a healthy body; often appended as a condition of signing a contract
Mutatis mutandis	change and change about
Nemine contradicente (nem. con.)	with no one speaking against
Nemo dat quod non habet (nemo dat)	no one can give what he does not have
Nolle prosequi	do not pursue
Non est factum	it is not his act (he didn't mean to do it)
Obiter dicta	incidental comments
Pari passu	of equal power
Prima facie	on the face of it
Per diem	by the day; an allowance paid businessmen to cover daily expenses while travelling
Pro rata	for the rate; divided in proportion
Pro tempore	for the time being; sometimes shortened to protem
Quantum meruit	as much as he deserves
Quid pro quo	something for something (you scratch my back, I'll scratch yours)
Ratio decidendi	the reason for deciding
Res ipsa loquitur	it speaks for itself
Sine die	without specifying a day
Sine qua non	without which, not (anything indispensable)
Sub judice	under adjudication
Sui generis	of its own kind
Uberrimae fidei	of the utmost good faith
Ultra vires	outside the permitted powers
Verbatim	word-for-word; a precise rendering of a discussion or text
Versus	against, often shortened to v.
Volenti non fit injuria	it is not a wrong if the person consents

Brand names that entered the language

Aspirin Bayer still owns the trademark for the acetylated derivative of salicylic acid in many countries around the world.

AstroTurf Commonly applied to any artificial grass surface. AstroTurf, developed by Monsanto industries, was originally called Chemgrass.

Band Aid The original plastic adhesive plaster was developed by Johnson & Johnson.

Breathalyser The instrument for police checks for alcohol consumed by a suspect driver is a trademark of Draeger Safety.

Coke The common name for any cola-based soft drink is still a trademark of Coca-Cola.

Frisbee Of the many varieties of flying disk available, only Wham-O owns the brand name and registered trademark of Frisbee.

Heroin The narcotic derived from synthesised opium was launched under the trademark by Bayer in 1898 and sold as a non-addictive morphine substitute and cough medicine for children.

Hoover Was once a synonym for vacuum cleaners and even made it as a verb. The Hoover Company has been making the devices since 1907.

Hula-Hoop The twirling hoop around hips or knees is a Hula-Hoop only if made by Wham-O.

Jacuzzi Only the whirlpool baths made by the company founded by Roy Jacuzzi can rightfully bear the name.

Jeep Rugged four-wheel drive vehicles may not bear the name unless they are made by Jeep, which began producing the original vehicles for the American army in the second world war. DaimlerChrysler now owns Jeep.

Kitty Litter Felines in search of relief

indoors must thank Edward Lowe, who invented the cat-box filler in 1947.

Kleenex The brand name of Kimberley-Clark's product has become synonymous with paper tissues around the world.

Muzak Anonymous, bland and faintly irritating background music heard in shops and other public places may only genuinely be called Muzak if produced by the South Carolina-based company of the same name.

Rollerblade The Rollerblade company that started the craze for in-line rollerskating can claim the trademark.

Scotch Tape Transparent cellophane adhesive tape is widely known as Scotch tape in America though the name is a trademark of the 3M company. In Britain the product is known as Sellotape, another brand name now owned by Henkel Consumer Adhesives.

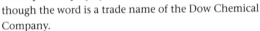

Styrofoam Expanded polystyrene is often called Styrofoam though the word is a trade name of the Dow Chemical Company.

Teflon The trade name for a solid, chemically inert polymer of tetrafluoroethylene manufactured by Dupont rather than any non-stick coating on cooking utensils.

Thermos The first vacuum flasks were made Germany in 1904 by Thermos GmbH. The tradename for their flasks is still registered.

Tupperware Plastic storage boxes produced by any firm other than the Tupperware Corporation have no right to take that name.

Vaseline Petroleum jelly produced by Unilever is known as Vaseline. Anything else is just plain petroleum jelly.

Walkman Mobile personal stereo systems not produced by Sony cannot properly bear the name.

Xerox Photocopiers of any stripe were routinely known as Xerox machines for many years. The financial plight of the company and its slide out of the world's offices has all but stopped the practice.

Acronyms: a selection

ABS	Asset backed security/Automated bond system
AG	German public company (Aktiengesellschaft)
AIM	Alternative Investment Market
APT	Arbitrage pricing theory
ARPU	Average revenue per user/unit
ARR	Accounting rate of return
ATEX	Atmosphere Explosif – EU Directive for equipment to be used in an explosive atmosphere
B2B	Business-to-business
B2C	Business-to-consumer
B2E	Business-to-education
B2G	Business-to-government
BDP	Best demonstrated practice
BPM	Business process management
BPR	Business process re-engineering
BV	Belgium/Netherlands limited liability company (Besloten Vennootschap)
CAE	Computer aided engineering
CAM	Computer aided manufacturing
CAP-M	Capital asset pricing model
CGMP	Current good manufacturing practice
CIE	Computer integrated enterprise
CMS	Content management system
CPMI	Computerised personnel management information
CQI	Continuous quality improvement
CRM	Customer relationship management
CWQI	Company wide quality improvement
DRM	Digital rights management
EAP	Employee assistance programme
EBIT	Earnings before interest and taxes
ECN	Electronic communications network
EPO	Enterprise profit optimisation
EPOS	Electronic point of sale
ERP	Enterprise resource planning
EVA	Economic value added
FMCG	Fast-moving consumer goods
FMS	Flexible manufacturing systems

GAAP	Generally accepted accounting principles
GmbH	German limited liability company (Gesellschaft mit beschränkter Haftung)
IBC	International business company – offshore company designation
IDB	Inter-American Development Bank
IPO	Initial public offering
ISIN	International Securities Identification Number
IWS	Integrated work stations
KK	Japanese joint stock company (Kabushiki Kaisha)
KM	Knowledge management
KPI	Key performance indicators
LAN	Local area network
MRP	Material requisition planning
NPV	Net present value
OJT	On-the-job training
OTC	Over-the-counter
P2P	Peer-to-peer
PLM	Product lifecycle management
R&D	Research and development
RTM	Route to market
SA	French limited company (Société anonyme)
SA	Spanish limited company (Sociedad anónima)
SBU	Strategic business unit
SCM	Supply chain management
SET	Secure electronic transaction
SHE	Safety, health and environment
SLA	Service level agreement
SME	Small and medium-sized enterprises
SpA	Italian limited company (Società per Azione)
SPC	Statistical process control
TLD	Top level domain – on the internet, something like a country code (.uk) or .com
URL	Uniform resource locator
USP	Unique selling point
VBM	Value-based management
WAP	Wireless application protocol
WEEE	Waste electrical and electronic equipmenrt

Business "jargon"

"Incomprehensible jargon is the hallmark of a profession," said Kingman Brewster, a former president of Yale University. He had in mind venerable professions such as medicine, the law and banking, professions whose practitioners have devised a language that is at times incomprehensible to all but other practitioners. He was not, in all probability, referring to the profession that arguably has the most jargon of them all: the management profession.

Managers gathered round the coffee machine say things to each other such as: "There's been a paradigm shift. We must identify new synergies for our organizational capabilities." No other manager is going to admit to not understanding what this means. The outsider, though, might wonder why they did not simply say: "Things have changed a lot lately. We need to do better in the future."

Problems start to arise when managers from different departments talk to each other. For each has its own sub-language, and these days the IT people have the richest. They want to talk in real time or offline, and they are limited only by their intellectual bandwidth. They are always talking about the drivers of their business (mainly digitisation), and they like to use leading-edge technology in order to create multifunctional new products and services that are networked throughout the organisation. Going forward, they're always in search of solutions, leading-edge solutions, that is.

> **they're always in search of solutions, leading-edge solutions, that is**

The human-resources folks, on the other hand, have issues on their agendas. They talk about the right skill sets, and doing 360-degree evaluations of the talent (sounds uncomfortable). Talent on the fast track these days has to be a good team player, or a knowledge harvester. Value creators have to work in cross-functional teams and try to put themselves in win-win situations, ones in which it seems to be possible for neither side to lose. Whatever that is, it's certainly not cricket.

For the marketing division today, everything is a brand. According to one typology, there is a familiarity brand, a distraction brand and a muscle brand. Brands are stretched, extended and built upon, while brand new brands are launched with carefully targeted campaigns. A niche brand has its own socio-economic dynamic. Of course.

Business jargon is susceptible to fashion. One of today's celebrated themes is risk. Managers know that there are no certainties any more, that everything is changing. Change is constant and increasing; they recite it like a mantra.

So too is risk. Everywhere managers look now they find risk – financial risk, structural risk, strategic risk, operational risk – the list is endless. All this risk has to be controlled in a pro-active value-creating way. One recent book has a chapter headed "Managing Programme Risk". Do not be misled. It has nothing to do with hanging on to pieces of paper at the theatre.

> **❝ all this risk has to be controlled in a pro-active value-creating way ❞**

Then there is knowledge. Managers live in a knowledge economy full of knowledge-intensive firms. Knowledge management is everybody's ideal core competence – although according to one author "we cannot understand KM (yes, it already has its own acronym) in terms of broad structural drivers." In what terms, you might be tempted to ask, can we understand it.

Acronyms are everywhere. Most of them are three-letter specimens (TQM, BPR, JIT, ABC, CRM, CIO and CTO, for a start), though occasionally the rarer two- and four-letter specimens can be found – IT and KM, for example, or MBWA and RFID. Some are known widely among managers, but some are home-made, a sort of secret code among a small exclusive group. "Told JP we'd do the FV before we head for LA", sort of thing.

Another fashionable subject with a rich seam of jargon is leadership. Leadership, we are told, is about empowerment and mastering capabilities. Management guru Tom Peters, in his latest book, *Re-Imagine*, says that leadership is "an act called conveying the Brand Promise via

> **❝ an act called conveying the Brand Promise via demonstrated High Conviction in pursuit of Great Purpose ❞**

demonstrated High Conviction in pursuit of Great Purpose."
Management writers love using capital letters; they think it helps
simple-minded readers get IT.

Leaders these days are forever making journeys. Often they are
journeys of self-discovery where they can relate to their inner
selves. Examples from history are frequently called upon. Famous
journey-takers, such as Alexander the Great and Shackleton, are
hardy favourites. One leadership book about Queen Elizabeth I
says that when the good queen "seemed to vacillate, it was likely
because the analytical and intuitive aspects of a pending decision
were not in sync in terms of the action itself or its timing." Does
that mean that the CEO of Elizabethan England Inc could not
make up her mind?

Jargon becomes a problem when managers fail to recognise times
when it is appropriate and times when it is not. What to make of
this, for example, taken from the home page of a very large service
company's web site: "Customized solutions boost employee
productivity and satisfaction, while supporting effective program
management and cost control. Our focus on service excellence,
technology investment, and Six Sigma measurement standards
ensures consistent results-driven performance. Clients receive
continual information on best practices, cost-reduction
opportunities, and competitive program enhancements, while our
consultants provide each employee with resourceful and
responsive personal advocacy." This is a sort of uber-jargon,
expressed in such an Orwellian dead-pan tone that it is not even
funny. The origin of the word "jargon" may well have been an
ancient word for the incomprehensible twittering of birds. There
are many birds that cannot twitter half so incomprehensibly as
this.

> **❝ each value stream within the operating system must be optimised individually from end to end ❞**

Management books (and, heaven
knows, there are enough of them –
some 3,000 business titles are
published every year in the United
States alone) can be excused for
indulging in some jargon, since
most of them are written for other managers. Even prize-winning
books do it. "Each value stream within the operating system must
be optimised individually from end to end," is a not untypical

sentence from a book called *Journey to Lean*, the winner of an award in 2004 from Britain's Management Consultancies Association.

A glance along a bookshelf of management writing throws up titles such as *Deep Smarts* which, in case you didn't guess, is "a potent form of experience-based wisdom that drives both organisational competitiveness and personal success"; and *The HR Value Proposition*, which shows how "HR creates value for internal stakeholders", without asking how painful that might be.

In *The Jargon of the Professions*, the book's author Kenneth Hudson writes that "not only do businessmen write pompous rubbish, they speak it as well." And they have been doing so for some time. He quotes a 1974 example of the chairman of a large British engineering concern who was asked in a television interview what he felt was the main problem of his company. His reply: "To generate the availability of exposure of our management."

> **not only do businessmen write pompous rubbish, they speak it as well**

Happily, some business writing is jargon-free, following George Orwell's advice to "never use a long word where a short one will do, and never use jargon if you can think of an everyday English equivalent". Among recent outstanding examples are Joan Magretta's *What Management Is*, and John Roberts's *The Modern Firm*. The *Harvard Business Review* too is a brave and dependable beacon in the dark and continually swirling fog of business gobbledegook. Caveat lector.

> **never use jargon if you can think of an everyday English equivalent**

Business laws and principles ✓

BENFORD'S LAW   In lists of numbers from many sources of data the leading digit 1 occurs much more often than the others (about 30% of the time). The law was discovered by Simon Newcomb, an American astronomer, in 1881. He noted that the first pages of books of logarithms were much more thumbed than others. Furthermore, the higher the digit, the less likely it is to occur. This applies to mathematical constants as much as utility bills, addresses, share prices, birth and death statistics, the height of mountains, etc.

BROOKS LAW   "Adding manpower to a late software project makes it later" said Fred Brooks, in his book *The Mythical Man-Month*.

GRESHAM'S LAW   "Bad money drives good money out of circulation." If coins of the same legal tender contain metal of different value, the coins composed of the cheaper metal will be used for payment, and those made of more expensive metal will be hoarded and disappear from circulation. Named after Sir Thomas Gresham (1519–79), a British financier and founder of the Royal Exchange.

MOORE'S LAW   "The number of transistors on a chip doubles every 18 months." An observation by Gordon Moore, a founder of Intel, regarding the pace of semiconductor technology development in 1961.

MURPHY'S LAW   Anything that can go wrong will go wrong.

PARKINSON'S LAW   "Work expands so as to fill the time available for its completion" was formulated by Cecil Northcote Parkinson in *The Economist* in 1955.

PARKINSON'S LAW OF DATA   Data expand to fill the space available for storage, so acquiring more memory will encourage the adoption of techniques that require more memory.

THE PETER PRINCIPLE   In a hierarchy, every employee tends to rise to his level of incompetence, according to Laurence Peter and Raymond Hull in their book of the same name published in 1969.

REILLY'S LAW This law of retail gravitation suggests that people are generally attracted to the largest shopping centre in the area. William Reilly, an American academic, proposed the law in a book published in 1931.

PARETO PRINCIPLE Also known as the 80/20 rule and named after Vilfredo Pareto (1848-1923), an Italian economist, who determined that 80% of activity comes from 20% of the people. The principle was extended (or simply misunderstood) by Joseph Juran, an American management guru, who suggested that for many phenomena 80% of consequences stem from 20% of the causes. That is, in many instances a large number of results stem from a small number of causes, eg, 80% of problems come from 20% of the equipment or workforce.

SAY'S LAW Aggregate supply creates its own aggregate demand. Attributed to Jean-Baptiste Say (1767–1832), a French economist. If output increases in a free-market economy, the sales would give the producers of the goods the same amount of income which would re-enter the economy and create demand for those goods. Keynes's law, attributed to John Maynard Keynes (1883–1946), a British economist, says that the opposite is true and that "demand creates its own supply" as businesses produce more to satisfy demand up to the limit of full employment.

Top business schools

EIU ranking, 2004

Northwestern University – Kellogg School of Management
Stanford Graduate School of Business
Dartmouth College – Tuck School of Business
Harvard Business School
IMD – International Institute for Management Development
University of Chicago – Graduate School of Business
Columbia Business School
University of Pennsylvania – Wharton School
IESE Business School – University of Navarra
New York University – Leonard Stern School of Business
University of Michigan – Business School
University of Virginia – Darden Graduate School of Business Administration
Duke University – Fuqua School of Business
Yale School of Management
Vlerick Leuven Gent Management School
Massachusetts Institute of Technology – MIT Sloan School of Management

Source: Economist Intelligence Unit

Financial Times ranking, 2004

University of Pennsylvania – Wharton School
Harvard Business School
Columbia Business School
INSEAD
London Business School
University of Chicago – Graduate School of Business
Stanford Graduate School of Business
New York University – Leonard Stern School of Business
Massachusetts Institute of Technology – MIT Sloan School of Management
Dartmouth College – Tuck School of Business
Northwestern University – Kellogg School of Management
IMD – International Institute for Management Development
IESE Business School – University of Navarra
Yale School of Management
IE – Instituto de Empresa
Cornell University – Johnson Graduate School of Management

Source: *Financial Times*

BusinessWeek ranking for US schools, 2004

Northwestern University – Kellogg School of Management
University of Chicago – Graduate School of Business
University of Pennsylvania – Wharton School
Stanford Graduate School of Business
Harvard Business School
University of Michigan – Business School
Cornell University – Johnson Graduate School of Management
Columbia Business School
Massachusetts Institute of Technology – MIT Sloan School of Management
Dartmouth College – Tuck School of Business

Source: *BusinessWeek*

BusinessWeek ranking for non-US schools, 2004

Queens University, Kingston, Ontario
IMD – International Institute for Management Development
INSEAD
ESADE
London Business School
Western Ontario
IESE Business School – University of Navarra
HEC-Paris
University of Toronto – Rotman
HEC-Montreal

Source: *BusinessWeek*

Some management styles

Management by exception – the policy of only looking closely at events that deviate significantly from an expected norm; for example, a drop in more than a certain percentage in sales revenue or a payment that is more than a specified number of days overdue.

Management by objectives – used to describe a management system whereby employees agree with their managers what their objectives are to be and then track progress in moving towards those objectives with their managers.

Management by walking about – most famously demonstrated by Hewlett-Packard, a computer firm, management by walking about is a style of management that emphasises the importance of face-to-face contact.

Managerial grid – a way to classify managerial styles by plotting "concern for results" against "concern for people", each on a scale of 1–9. For example:

1,1 the impoverished style – only concerned to get the necessary work done with the minimum effort

9,1 the scientific management style – where there is a concentration on maximising efficiency

5,5 the middle of the road style – where the aim is to get reasonable results and keep people reasonably happy

9,9 the team management style – where everyone works together to get the best out of themselves and others.

DIGITAL **assistants**

Shipments of BlackBerry-type devices, '000

	2002	2003	2004
US	327	479	1,985
Worldwide	363	600	2,592

Shipments of PDAs, '000

	2002	2003	2004
US	6,049	5,066	3,751
Western Europe	1,998	2,455	2,848
Asia/Pacific	2,262	1,596	1,279
Japan	898	484	270
Rest of world	1,414	972	1,257
Total	12,621	10,573	9,405

Source: IDC

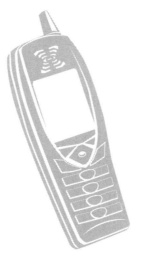

Laptops and PCs

Worldwide PC unit shipments by region

Region	2002	2003	2004
Asia Pacific	25,667,446	29,447,296	34,326,368
Canada	3,051,000	3,303,644	3,845,600
Central/eastern Europe	6,463,419	8,084,934	10,283,046
Japan	12,467,800	12,815,892	13,399,704
Latin America	7,589,681	7,928,596	10,315,198
Middle East/Africa	3,938,278	4,923,652	6,323,054
US	47,550,968	52,698,932	58,248,284
Western Europe	31,655,320	35,961,248	42,040,712
Total	138,383,904	155,164,192	178,781,952

Worldwide portable PC unit shipments by region

Region	2002	2003	2004
Asia Pacific	3,366,566	4,762,591	6,156,397
Canada	640,600	756,800	1,006,900
Central/eastern Europe	482,446	794,031	1,488,416
Japan	6,161,914	6,256,300	6,544,589
Latin America	542,832	635,866	850,394
Middle East/Africa	416,331	728,769	1,152,694
US	10,883,296	13,807,702	16,623,580
Western Europe	8,326,028	11,640,576	15,265,436
Total	30,820,012	39,382,632	49,088,404

Source: IDC Worldwide Quarterly PC Tracker, 2005

Chip power

	Transistors, m	Processor
1971	0.00225	4004
1972	0.0025	8008
1973		
1974	0.005	8080
1975		
1976		
1977		
1978	0.029	8086
1979		
1980		
1981		
1982	0.12	286
1983		
1984		
1985	0.275	Intel386
1986		
1987		
1988		
1989	1.18	Intel486
1990		
1991		
1992		
1993	3.1	Pentium
1994		
1995		
1996		
1997	7.5	Pentium II
1998		
1999	24	Pentium III
2000	42	Pentium 4
2001		
2002	220	Itanium
2003	410	Itanium 2

Source: Intel

The impact of software piracy

Losses by region, 2003

	$bn
Western Europe	9.60
Asia Pacific	7.55
US & Canada	7.23
Eastern Europe	2.11
Latin America	1.27
Middle East & Africa	1.03

Losses by country, 2003

	$bn
US	6.50
China	3.82
France	2.31
Germany	1.90
Japan	1.63
UK	1.60
Italy	1.13
Russia	1.10
Canada	0.74
Netherlands	0.58
Brazil	0.52
Spain	0.51
South Korea	0.46
Mexico	0.37
India	0.37
Australia	0.34
Poland	0.30
Switzerland	0.29
Sweden	0.24
Belgium	0.24

Sources: International Data Corporation (IDC); Business Software Alliance (BSA)

Spam and e-mail

Leading spam-producing countries

2004	% of total
US	42.11
South Korea	13.43
China (incl. Hong Kong)	8.44
Canada	5.71
Brazil	3.34
Japan	2.57
France	1.37
Spain	1.18
UK	1.13
Germany	1.03
Taiwan	1.00
Mexico	0.89
Others	17.80

Source: Sophos

You have junk mail

Spam and e-mail facts, 2004

Daily e-mails sent	31bn
Daily e-mails sent per e-mail address	56
Daily e-mails sent per person	174
Daily e-mails sent per corporate user	34
Daily e-mails received per person	10
E-mail addresses per person	3.1 (average)
Cost to all internet users	$255m
E-mail considered spam	40%
Daily spam e-mails sent	12.4bn
Daily spam received per person	6
Annual spam received per person	2,200
Spam cost to all US corporations (2002)	$8.9bn
Corporate e-mail considered spam	15–20%

Source: InsideSpam.com

Internet suffixes

Afghanistan	.af	Cambodia	.kh
Albania	.al	Cameroon	.cm
Algeria	.dz	Canada	.ca
American Samoa	.as	Cape Verde	.cv
Andorra	.ad	Cayman Islands	.ky
Angola	.ao	Central African Rep.	.cf
Anguilla	.ai	Chad	.td
Antarctica	.aq	Chile	.cl
Antigua & Barbuda	.ag	China	.cn
Argentina	.ar	Christmas Island	.cx
Armenia	.am	Cocos (Keeling) Islands	.cc
Aruba	.aw	Colombia	.co
Ascension Island	.ac	Comoros	.km
Australia	.au	Congo (Democratic	
Austria	.at	Republic of Congo)	.cd
Azerbaijan	.az	Congo-Brazzaville	
Bahamas	.bs	(Republic of Congo)	.cg
Bahrain	.bh	Cook Islands	.ck
Bangladesh	.bd	Costa Rica	.cr
Barbados	.bb	Côte d'Ivoire	.ci
Belarus	.by	Croatia	.hr
Belgium	.be	Cuba	.cu
Belize	.bz	Cyprus	.cy
Benin	.bj	Czech Republic	.cz
Bermuda	.bm	Denmark	.dk
Bhutan	.bt	Djibouti	.dj
Bolivia	.bo	Dominica	.dm
Bosnia	.ba	Dominican Republic	.do
Botswana	.bw	East Timor	.tp
Bouvet Island	.bv	Ecuador	.ec
Brazil	.br	Egypt	.eg
British Indian Ocean		El Salvador	.sv
Territory	.io	Equatorial Guinea	.gq
Brunei	.bn	Eritrea	.er
Bulgaria	.bg	Estonia	.ee
Burkina Faso	.bf	Ethiopia	.et
Burundi	.bi	Falkland Islands	.fk

Faroe Islands	.fo	Jersey	.je
Fiji	.fj	Jordan	.jo
Finland	.fi	Kazakhstan	.kz
France	.fr	Kenya	.ke
French Guyana	.gf	Kirgizstan	.kg
French Polynesia	.pf	Kiribati	.ki
French Southern Territories	.tf	Kuwait	.kw
Gabon	.ga	Laos	.la
Gambia, The	.gm	Latvia	.lv
Georgia	.ge	Lebanon	.lb
Germany	.de	Lesotho	.ls
Ghana	.gh	Liberia	.lr
Gibraltar	.gi	Libya	.ly
Greece	.gr	Liechtenstein	.li
Greenland	.gl	Lithuania	.lt
Grenada	.gd	Luxembourg	.lu
Guadeloupe	.gp	Macau	.mo
Guam	.gu	Macedonia	.mk
Guatemala	.gt	Madagascar	.mg
Guernsey	.gg	Malawi	.mw
Guinea	.gn	Malaysia	.my
Guinea-Bissau	.gw	Maldives	.mv
Guyana	.gy	Mali	.ml
Haiti	.ht	Malta	.mt
Heard & McDonald		Marshall Islands	.mh
Islands	.hm	Martinique	.mq
Honduras	.hn	Mauritania	.mr
Hong Kong	.hk	Mauritius	.mu
Hungary	.hu	Mayotte	.yt
Iceland	.is	Mexico	.mx
India	.in	Micronesia	.fm
Indonesia	.id	Moldova	.md
Iran	.ir	Monaco	.mc
Iraq	.iq	Mongolia	.mn
Ireland	.ie	Monserrat	.ms
Isle of Man	.im	Morocco	.ma
Israel	.il	Mozambique	.mz
Italy	.it	Myanmar	.mm
Jamaica	.jm	Namibia	.na
Japan	.jp	Nauru	.nr

Nepal	.np
Netherlands	.nl
Netherlands Antilles	.an
New Caledonia	.nc
New Zealand	.nz
Nicaragua	.ni
Niger	.ne
Nigeria	.ng
Niue	.nu
Norfolk Island	.nf
North Korea (Democratic People's Republic of Korea)	.kp
Northern Mariana Islands	.mp
Norway	.no
Oman	.om
Pakistan	.pk
Palau	.pw
Palestinian Territories	.ps
Panama	.pa
Papua New Guinea	.pg
Paraguay	.py
Peru	.pe
Philippines	.ph
Pitcairn	.pn
Poland	.pl
Portugal	.pt
Puerto Rico	.pr
Qatar	.qa
Réunion	.re
Romania	.ro
Russia	.ru
Rwanda	.rw
St Helena	.sh
St Kitts & Nevis	.kn
St Lucia	.lc
St Pierre & Miquelon	.pm
St Vincent & the Grenadines	.vc
Samoa	.ws

San Marino	.sm
São Tomé and Príncipe	.st
Saudi Arabia	.sa
Senegal	.sn
Seychelles	.sc
Serbia & Montenegro	.yu
Sierra Leone	.sl
Singapore	.sg
Slovakia	.sk
Slovenia	.si
Solomon Islands	.sb
Somalia	.so
South Africa	.za
South Korea (Republic of Korea)	.kr
South Georgia and the South Sandwich Islands	.gs
Spain	.es
Sri Lanka	.lk
Sudan	.sd
Suriname	.sr
Svalbard & Jan Mayen Islands	.sj
Swaziland	.sz
Sweden	.se
Switzerland	.ch
Syria	.sy
Taiwan	.tw
Tajikistan	.tj
Tanzania	.tz
Thailand	.th
Togo	.tg
Tokelau	.tk
Tonga	.to
Trinidad & Tobago	.tt
Tunisia	.tn
Turkey	.tr
Turkmenistan	.tm
Turks & Caicos Islands	.tc
Tuvalu	.tv

Uganda	.ug	Aviation	.aero
Ukraine	.ua	Business organisations	.biz
United Arab Emirates	.ae	Commercial	.com
United Kingdom	.uk	Co-operative	
United States	.us	organisations	.coop
United States Minor		Educational	.edu
Outlying Islands	.um	US government	.gov
Uruguay	.uy	Open TLD	
Uzbekistan	.uz	(Top level domain)	.info
Vanuatu	.vu	International	
Vatican	.va	organisations	.int
Venezuela	.ve	US Department of	
Vietnam	.vn	Defence	.mil
Virgin Islands, British	.vg	Museums	.museum
Virgin Islands, US	.vi	Personal	.name
Wallis & Futuna Islands	.wf	Networks	.net
Western Sahara	.eh	Organisations	.org
Yemen	.ye		
Zaire	.cd		
Zambia	.zm		
Zimbabwe	.zw		

Source: Internet Assigned Numbers Authority

The corporate **high** life

Aircraft ownership by Fortune 500 companies

2004	No.	%
Light jets	8	0.5%
Medium jets	729	47.4%
Heavy jets	549	35.7%
Twin turbine helicopters	100	6.5%
Single turbine helicopters	54	3.5%
Light turboprops	87	5.7%
Heavy turboprops	11	0.7%
Total aircraft	1,538	

Worldwide business fleets

2004	World total	North America	Europe	Asia & Middle East	Oceania
Jets	12,974	9,754	1,470	461	86
Turboprops	10,147	6896	905	392	199

Average age of worldwide business aicraft

2004	Years
Heavy jet	14.09
Medium jet	16.81
Light jet	16.41
Heavy turboprop	34.05
Medium turboprop	21.82
Light turboprop	7.11

Source: AvDataInc

Big airlines

Total scheduled passengers carried

2003	m		m
American Airlines	88.8	Air France	43.3
Delta Air Lines	84.1	All Nippon Airways	43.4
United Airlines	66.5	US Airways	41.3
Northwest Airlines	52.8	Continental Airlines	38.5
Lufthansa	44.5	British Airways	34.8

Note: Includes domestic and international travel of IATA members.

Source: International Air Transport Association

Total fleet

2004	No. of aircraft		No. of aircraft
American Airlines	783	Japan Airlines	190
Federal Express	641	KLM	164
Delta Air Lines	550	Iberia	149
United Airlines	532	All Nippon Airways	149
Northwest Airlines	464	Saudi Arabian Airlines	146
Air France	351	Qantas	144
Continental Airlines	342	America West Airlines	139
Lufthansa	333	Air China	129
British Airways	302	Korean Air Lines	121
US Airways	279	Alitalia	115
United Parcel Service	257	Singapore Airlines	115
Air Canada	208	Alaska Airlines	110
China Southern Airlines	203		

Source: International Air Transport Association

Plane speaking

Busiest airports

2004	Total passengers, m		Total cargo, m tonnes
Atlanta, Hartsfield	83.6	Memphis, Intl.	3.55
Chicago, O'Hare	75.5	Hong Kong, Intl.	3.13
London, Heathrow	67.3	Anchorage, Intl.	2.37
Tokyo, Haneda	62.3	Tokyo, Narita	2.37
Los Angeles, Intl.	60.7	Seoul, Inchon	2.13
Dallas, Ft. Worth	59.4	Los Angeles, Intl.	1.90
Frankfurt, Main	51.1	Frankfurt, Main	1.84
Paris, Charles de Gaulle	50.9	Singapore, Changi	1.80
Amsterdam, Schiphol	42.5	Miami, Intl.	1.78
Denver, Intl.	42.4	Louisville, Standiford Fd.	1.74

Source: Airports Council International

Airport journeys by cab

	Cost, $ (estimate)	Distance, km	Time, minutes	Airport
Tokyo	240	60	80	Narita
London	110	25	40	Heathrow
Hong Kong	50	30	50	Chek Lap Kok
New York	45	25	50	JFK
Singapore	18	20	20	Changi

Sources: *The Economist*; Mid-Tokyo Maps

Air miles to go

	Total awarded, cumulative, bn	Total unredeemed, cumulative, bn
1981	4.1	2.2
1982	20.9	6.1
1983	59.2	15.8
1984	124.3	39.0
1985	218.6	76.0
1986	342.4	127.0
1987	505.4	208.7
1988	787.5	400.0
1989	1,125.1	617.2
1990	1,519.2	877.9
1991	1,962.5	1,165.9
1992	2,461.3	1,486.1
1993	3,044.3	1,867.1
1994	3,688.3	2,232.4
1995	4,349.3	2,608.6
1996	5,179.3	3,183.3
1997	6,159.3	3,891.5
1998	7,279.3	4,608.5
1999	8,569.3	5,539.7
2000	10,009.3	6,630.2
2001	11,609.3	7,888.6
2002	13,255.3	9,131.7

Source: WebFlyer

Ship ahoy

Merchant fleets

2004	By country of registration, gross tonnage		By country of ownership, gross tonnage, m
Panama	131.5	Greece	90.4
Liberia	53.9	Japan	80.6
Bahamas	35.4	Germany	42.9
Greece	32	US	36.9
Singapore	26.3	China	36.2
Hong Kong	26.1	Norway	32.4
Malta	22.4	Hong Kong	26.2
Cyprus	21.3	South Korea	18
China	20.4	Taiwan	15.6
Norway	15.4	UK	14.6

Source: Lloyd's Register

The world's largest cruise ships

2004	m^3	Passenger capacity	Cruising line
Queen Mary II	4,248	2,800	Cunard
Adventures of the Seas	4,021	3,114	RCI
Explorer of the Seas	4,021	3,114	RCI
Navigator of the Seas	4,021	3,114	RCI
Mariner of the Seas	4,021	3,114	RCI
Voyager of the Seas	4,021	3,114	RCI
Caribbean Princess	3,285	3,100	Princess
Diamond Princess	3,200	2,600	Princess
Sapphire Princess	3,200	2,670	Princess
Superstar Sagittarius II	3,172	3,000	Star
Superstar Capricorn	3,172	3,000	Star
Carnival Conquest	3,115	2,974	Carnival
Carnival Glory	3,115	2,976	Carnival
Carnival Valor	3,115	2,976	Carnival
Crown Princess	3,115	2,600	Princess

Source: Cruise2.com

The age of the train?

Most rail use

2003	Km per person	Rail freight, m tonnes-km	
Japan	1,891	US	2,264,982
Switzerland	1,751	Russia	1,664,300
Belarus	1,344	China	1,647,558
France	1,203	India	353,194
Ukraine	1,100	Canada	311,371
Russia	1,080	Ukraine	225,287
Austria	1,008	Kazakhstan	148,370
Denmark	999	Senegal	105,725
Netherlands	855	South Africa	105,719
Germany	842	Germany	73,973

Source: Union Internationale des Chemins de Fer

The world's fastest rail runs

2003	Departure	Arrival	Distance, km	Speed, km/h
Japan	Kokura	Hiroshima	192.0	261.8
France	Valence TGV	Avignon TGV	129.7	259.4
International	Brussels Midi	Valence TGV	831.3	242.1
Germany	Frankfurt Flughafen	Siegburg/Bonn	143.3	232.4
Spain	Madrid Atocha	Sevilla	470.5	209.1
Sweden	Alvesta	Hässleholm	98.0	178.2
UK	York	Darlington	71.0	177.5
Italy	Roma Termini	Firenze SMN	261.0	166.6
US	Wilmington	Baltimore	110.1	165.1
Finland	Salo	Karjaa	53.1	151.7
China	Shenzhen	Guangzhou Dong	139.0	151.6

Source: *Railway Gazette International*

Pedal p🚲wer

Worldwide bicycle production was 11m in 1950, 20m in 1960, 36m in 1970, 62m in 1980, 91m in 1990 and 104m in 2002. The high point was in 1988, when 105m units were produced.

China is the largest producer, with 63m bikes in 2002, 23% more than in 2001 and 61% of the world total, and 73m estimated for 2003. China's production has climbed from 42.7m in 1999 and 52.2m in 2000, with a dip to 51.2m in 2001.

As Chinese production has risen, other large producers – Japan, Taiwan and the United States – have experienced a decline. Production in Taiwan fell from 8.4m units in 1999 (7.8m exported) to 4.4 in 2002 (4.2m exported); in America from 1.7m in 1999 to 0.41m in 2002; and in Japan from 5.6m in 1999 to 3.08m in 2002.

Around 46m of China's 2002 total of 63m was exported (up from 22.7m in 1999), with the United States the largest customer, taking 18.6m units (from an import total of 19.3m).

Vietnam was the fastest-growing producer in 2002, producing 2m units, a 250% increase compared with 2001.

In prospering Asian nations, bicycle usage is declining as car fleets grow. In America (where car travel remains cheap) trips to work by bike fell from 0.5% in 1980 to an even tinier 0.4% in 2000.

Estimates of the number of bikes in Beijing, China's capital, range from 4m to 10m, and in 2004, the 4-yuan annual tax on bikes was dropped. However, as car numbers increase by 20,000 per month, bike journeys are estimated to have dropped by 60% in ten years.

By 2005, 1,250 former rail corridors in the United States had been converted to cycle trails (a total of 12,650 miles). In 2004 the total was 1,212 (12,585 miles) and in 1988 it was 198 (359 miles).

Health-care providers in Africa are increasingly using bicycles, especially for delivery of immunisation programmes. Two projects in Senegal reported a 58% increase in speed by nurses using cycles on their rounds rather than walking, and a saving of 40c per journey compared with those using taxis.

Germany and the Netherlands lead the way in cycle-friendly safety measures, such as cycle paths, traffic calming and urban design. Cyclists in America are twice as likely to be killed as those in Germany, and more than three times as likely as cyclists in the Netherlands.

Cyclist deaths in America have fallen over the past 25 years, but only because numbers of cyclists – particularly children – have dropped. The percentage of children walking or cycling to school has dropped from 71% to 18% over a generation.

Cycling accounts for less than 2% of trips in the UK, compared with 10% in Sweden, 11% in Germany, 15% in Switzerland and 18% in Denmark. British government tax measures to promote cycling include the ability to claim tax relief of up to 20p per mile cycled in the course of business – excluding travel to and from work.

In the Netherlands, a population of just over 16m is estimated to own 17m bikes, with 3.4m daily commutes being made by bike. Bicycle theft in Amsterdam is estimated at around 180,000 per year.

Sources: World Watch Institute; *Bicycle Retailer and Industry News*, *The Guardian*

Inventors and inventions

1450 Leon Battista Alberti, an Italian philosopher, architect, musician, painter and sculptor from Genoa, invented the first mechanical anemometer.

1756 John Smeaton, a British engineer, made concrete by adding aggregate to cement. In 1824, Joseph Aspdin, another Briton, invented Portland cement by burning ground limestone and clay together. In 1867, Joseph Monier, a French gardener, patented the idea of reinforced concrete.

1830 Edwin Beard Budding, an engineer from Stroud in Gloucestershire, was awarded the first patent for a mechanical lawn mower.

1843 Alexander Bain, a Scottish clockmaker, patented the fax machine – 33 years before a patent was granted for the telephone. The first commercial fax service was opened between Paris and Lyon in 1865.

1849 Walter Hunt, a New York inventor, received a patent for the safety pin.

1851 Elias Howe patented an Automatic Continuous Clothing Closure but took the invention no further. In 1896, Whitcomb Judson marketed the Clasp Locker, a hook-and-eye shoe fastener. In 1913, Gideon Sundback, a Swedish-born electrical engineer living in Canada, improved the Judson C-curity Fastener and came up with the modern zip.

1861 Elisha Otis patented the "Improvement in Hoisting Apparatus". Lifts had been in use for some time but Otis invented a safety mechanism that stopped the lift falling if the rope broke, thus opening the way for safe passenger lifts and allowing the development of the high-rise building.

1866 George McGill developed the Patent Single Stroke Staple Press to insert brass fasteners into papers. In 1895 the Jones Manufacturing Company of Norwalk, Connecticut, introduced the first stapler that used steel staples formed into a continuous strip.

1872 **Aaron Montgomery Ward** sent out the world's first mail-order catalogue for his Chicago-based business.

1873 **Joseph Glidden**, a farmer from De Kalb, Illinois, applied for a patent on barbed wire.

1873 **Levi Strauss**, a Bavarian immigrant who had travelled to California during the Gold Rush, and Jacob Davis, a tailor from Reno, Nevada, got a patent for trousers strengthened with rivets to make sturdy workwear. Soon after they began to produce the first blue denim jeans.

1876 **Alexander Graham Bell** unveiled his "electrical speech machine" in Boston, Massachusetts, later to become known as the telephone, making the first ever phone call to his assistant: "Mr Watson, come here, I want you." He filed for a patent on the invention hours before a competitor, Elisha Grey. Though neither had produced a working telephone at the time, Bell's device controversially incorporated elements of his competitor's phone that had not appeared in his original patent.

> **the first ever phone call was 'Mr Watson, come here, I want you'**

1877 **Thomas Edison** invented the tin-foil phonograph. Alexander Graham Bell's graphophone of 1883 employed a wax cylinder which could be played many times but required separate sound recording for each cylinder. In 1887, Emile Berliner, a German immigrant working in Washington, DC, was granted a patent for the gramophone on which multiple, reproducable, pre-recorded flat-disc records could be played.

1879 **Thomas Edison** invented the first practical electric light bulb. Though the idea was not new no one had previously managed to produce a bulb that was cheap and robust enough for mass production.

1883 **James Ritty and John Birch** got a patent for the first mechanical cash register, invented for use in Ritty's saloon in Dayton, Ohio.

1888 **Marvin Stone** of Washington, DC, patented a spiral-winding process to manufacture the first wax-coated paper drinking straws.

1888 **Thomas Edison** filed a patent for the Kinetoscope, the forerunner of the modern motion-picture camera.

inventors and inventions *continued*

1891 James Naismith, a Canadian physical-education instructor, invented basketball.

1895 Charles Fey, a San Francisco car mechanic, invented the first mechanical fruit machine, the Liberty Bell.

1895 Guglielmo Marconi sent wireless signals over a mile at his laboratory in Italy. The next year, in Britain, he was granted the world's first patent for a system of wireless telegraphy.

1899 Johan Vaaler, a Norwegian inventor, was granted a patent for the paperclip in Germany. His design never really caught on as the Gem paperclip (the type most common today) was already in production in Britain.

1903 Albert Parkhouse, an employee of Timberlake Wire and Novelty Company in Jackson, Michigan, invented a coat hanger made from a piece of bent wire with the ends twisted together to form a hook. Colleagues had apparently complained that the firm provided insufficient coat storage.

1908 Jacques Brandenberger, a Swiss engineer working for a French textile company, invented Cellophane.

1921 Earle Dickson, a cotton-buyer at Johnson & Johnson, invented the Band-Aid self-adhesive plaster.

1921 John Larson, a medical student at the University of California, invented the polygraph, a lie-detecting machine.

1927 Erik Rotheim, a Norwegian, patented the first aerosol can that dispensed products using a propellant system.

1930 Scotch tape, the world's first transparent cellophane adhesive tape, was introduced. It was invented by Richard Drew, an engineer at 3M, a company located in St Paul, Minnesota. John Borden, another 3M engineer, invented the tape dispenser with a built-in cutter in 1932.

1932 Carlton Cole Magee invented the first parking meter in response to the growing problem of parking congestion in Oklahoma City. They were first installed there three years later.

1934 **Percy Shaw**, a 23-year-old British inventor, patented cats eyes to assist driving in fog or at night.

1938 **Laszlo Biro**, a Hungarian journalist, invented the ballpoint pen.

1938 **Polytetrafluoroethylene** (or PTFE) was discovered by Roy Plunkett at DuPont's research facility in New Jersey. PTFE was first marketed as Teflon in 1945.

1940 **Norman Breakey** of Toronto invented the paint roller.

1942 **Cyanoacrylate** was invented by Harry Coover at the Kodak Research Laboratories while developing a plastic for gunsights. The product was not considered for commercial application until 1958 and later became known as superglue.

1947 **The transistor** was invented at Bell Telephone Laboratories by a team led by physicists John Bardeen, Walter Brattain and William Shockley. In 1958, Jack Kilby of Texas Instruments unveiled the integrated circuit, but in 1959 Fairchild Semiconductor filed a patent for a semiconductor integrated circuit invented by Robert Noyce, starting a ten-year legal battle over who had invented the chip. In 1968, Ted Hoff, an employee of Intel, invented the microprocessor. In 1970, Doug Engelbart received a patent for his "X-Y position indicator for a display system", which was developed into the computer mouse. In 1976, Steve Jobs and Steve Wozniak made a microprocessor computer board called Apple I and a year after introduced the Apple II, the world's first personal computer.

> **❝...starting a ten-year battle over who had invented the chip ❞**

1951 **George de Mestral** patented Velcro. The Swiss engineer, a keen mountaineer and inventor, noticed how burrs attached themselves to his clothes and his dog's fur and developed the idea for his new fastener.

1952 **Joseph Woodland and Bernard Silver**, graduate students at the Drexel Institute of Technology in Philadelphia, were issued a patent for the forerunner of the bar code.

inventors and inventions *continued*

1953 Norm Larsen, a chemist, made many attempts to develop an anti-corrosion formula working on the principle of water displacement in his lab in San Diego, California. In 1953, he succeeded and WD-40 (standing for water displacement 40th attempt) was born.

1954 Dee Horton and Lew Hewitt invented the automatic sliding door in Corpus Christi, Texas. The first door that entered service in 1960 was a unit donated to the City of Corpus Christi.

1955 Eugene Polley, an engineer working for America's Zenith Corporation, created the Flash-matic, the first wireless television remote control.

1956 Christopher Cockerell, a British engineer, invented the hovercraft.

1956 Bette Nesmith Graham, a secretary in Dallas, Texas, sold the first batch of Mistake Out, a liquid correcting fluid. Some years later, the product much improved, it was renamed Liquid Paper.

1958 Alfred Neustadter from Brooklyn, New York, first marketed the Rolodex, a rotating index-card holder.

1959 Ernie Fraze invented the easy-open ring-pull can in Kettering, Ohio, reputedly after struggling to open a can of beer at a family picnic.

1965 James Russell was granted 22 patents relating to his compact-disk system. CDs only came into wide use after they were taken up by Philips, a Dutch electronics firm, in 1980.

1965 James Faria and Robert Wright of Monsanto Industries filed a patent for a monofilament ribbon surface that would later become Astro Turf.

1968 Spencer Silver, a researcher at 3M looking into improving adhesives, came up with a new glue that produced a very weak bond. Art Fry, another researcher, who had often become frustrated when bookmarks fell out of his hymnal in church, eventually came up with a use for the product. Post-it notes were introduced in 1980.

1968 Roy Jacuzzi invented the first self-contained whirlpool bath with built-in water jets.

1979 Gordon Matthews's firm VMX (Voice Message Express) in Dallas, Texas, applied for a patent for the first voicemail system, which he then sold to 3M.

1981 IBM launched the first personal computer complete with a new operating system developed by a fledgling software company, the "Microsoft disk operating system" or MS-DOS.

1983 Microsoft announced that its new operating system would be on sale by the next year. Though originally called Interface Manager, the product was soon renamed Windows.

1988 Bryan Molloy and Klaus Schmiegel invented a class of aryloxyphenylpropylamines which included fluoxetine hydrochloride. It was the active ingredient in Eli Lilly's new drug, Prozac, the world's most widely used antidepressant.

❝Prozac, the world's most widely used antidepressant❞

1989 Tim Berners-Lee, a British scientist at CERN, a particle physics laboratory in Switzerland, developed a system to ease the sharing of databases and information. In 1990, he created the hypertext transfer protocol (HTTP) to allow computers to communicate over the internet. He also designed the Uniform Resource Locator (URL) to give sites addresses on the internet and invented a browser program to retrieve hypertext documents called the world wide web (WWW).

Famous patents

Invention	Year patented	Who by
Cotton gin	1794	Eli Whitney
Rubber vulcanisation	1844	Charles Goodyear
Manner of buoying vessels	1849	Abraham Lincoln
Elevator brake	1861	Elisha Graves Otis
Cast steel plough	1865	John Deere
Typewriter	1868	Christopher Sholes
Telephone/telegraphy	1876	Alexander Graham Bell
Statue of Liberty	1879	Auguste Bartholdi
Electric light	1880	Thomas Alva Edison
Electric light	1881	Lewis Howard Latimer
Punch-card tabulator	1889	Herman Hollerith
Radio	1897	Guglielmo Marconi
Internal-combustion engine	1898	Rudolf Diesel
Asprin	1900	Felix Hoffmann
Electric railway	1901	Granville T Woods
Air conditioner	1906	Willis Haviland Carrier
Flying machine	1906	Orville and Wilbur Wright
Automobile	1911	Henry Ford
X-ray tube	1916	William D. Coolidge
Diving suit	1921	Harry Houdini
Traffic signal	1923	Garrett A. Morgan
Paint and stain/process of producing same	1925	George Washington Carver
Climbing rose (first plant patented)	1931	Henry F. Bosenberg
Electrophotography (Xerox)	1939	Chester F. Carlson
Flourescent lamp	1939	Edmund Germer
Polyurethane	1942	William E. Hanford/Donald F. Holmes
Television receiver	1948	Louis W. Parker
Transistor	1950	John Bardeen/Walter H. Brattain/ William B. Shockley

Invention	Year patented	Who by
Oral contraceptive	1954	Frank B. Colton
Nuclear fission	1955	Enrico Fermi
Pulse transfer controlling devices (magnetic core memory forerunner)	1955	An Wang
Video tape recording	1955	Charles P. Ginsburg
Random Access Memory (RAM)	1956	Jay W. Forrester
Polypropylene plastics	1958	Robert Banks/Paul Hogan
Laser	1960	Arthur Shawlow/Charles Townes
Safety belt	1962	Nils I. Bohlin
Computer mouse	1970	Douglas Engelbert
Optical fibres	1972	Donald Keck/Robert Maurer/ Peter Schultz
Knee implant prosthsesis	1975	Ysidro M. Martinez
Personal computer	1979	Steve Wozniak
Genetic engineering	1980	Herb Boyer/Stan Cohen
Prozac	1982	Bryan B. Molloy/Klaus Schmiegel
Transgenic non-human mammals (first animal patent – "The mouse that went to Harvard")	1988	Philip Leder

Sources: United States Patent and Trademarks Office; National Inventors' Hall of Fame

Business etiquette tips

Business cards

In Asia and East Asia, the giving and receiving of business cards is a formal affair. Offer your card with both hands, and accept graciously those you are handed (do not shove them into a pocket).

In Japan, have a business card (a *meishi*) with you at all times. Failure to offer one signals that you are not interested in pursuing the relationship.

When visiting China or Japan, have your business cards printed in English on one side and Chinese or Japanese on the other.

Names and titles and status

In Japan, although things are changing, be cautious about calling people by their first name – first names are often restricted to family and very close friends. In general, it's best to couple someone's last name with "san" (for example, Koizumi-*san*) – this works for both men and women.

> " Germans are much friendlier if you appreciate their educational credentials "

Germans like to be called by titles, such as doctor or professor, and will prove much friendlier if you appear to appreciate their educational credentials.

When entering a taxi in Japan, the most important person sits in the middle with an acolyte on either side.

Communication

When in China or Japan, don't be unnerved by silences – pauses in conversation are an important part of communication.

Falling asleep in meetings or presentations is not uncommon in Japan. Closed eyes can also be a sign of concentration.

In Thailand, a simple bow of the head is preferable to a handshake. The traditional "wai" (hands in prayer position while bowing) is governed by strict etiquette rules and best avoided.

> **" the woes of public transport are a surefire way of reviving conversation "**

In London, the woes of public transport are a sure-fire way of reviving flagging conversation.

Like many Germans, Berliners tend to be earnest and straightforward. It is best to say exactly what you mean and to keep attempts at humour out of business meetings. Irony can be taken the wrong way.

Deadlines and punctuality

In France, the quality of a product and the persuasiveness of an argument are far more important than the setting of deadlines.

In Germany and Switzerland, always try to be on time or, if possible, early to appointments, and arrange for meetings or interviews well in advance.

Muslims answer the call to prayer five times a day. Long meetings in the Arab world may be interrupted accordingly.

In Japan, don't expect an immediate response to anything. Decisions are usually made collectively, and answers typically take much longer than in western companies. Once a decision is taken in Japan, however, the machine rolls forward smoothly and action is speedy.

Definite no-nos

In Arab countries, male business travellers should avoid flirting with local women.

In Japan, do not leave your chopsticks standing upright in a bowl of rice: this resembles a Buddhist funerary custom.

When in Russia, don't shake hands through a doorway, light a cigarette from a candle, bring an even number of flowers, or whistle indoors.

Don't boast about your past when visiting California. Here, your pedigree counts for less than your next big idea.

Eating and drinking

Breakfast meetings are rare in London. Most Brits subscribe to Oscar Wilde's claim that "only dull people are interesting at breakfast".

business etiquette tips *continued*

In France, to refuse wine at a business lunch would be permissible, but to refuse it at a dinner could be considered rude.

In Russia, always hand in your coat at the cloakroom when visiting a restaurant – draping it over the back of your chair is frowned upon.

When in Italy, order an espresso after eating. Topping off a meal with a frothy cappuccino would be unthinkable to a native.

> **" in Japan, never blow your nose on the *oshibori* ""**

In Japan, never blow your nose on the *oshibori* (a tightly rolled hot towel).

According to German superstition, if you don't look into another person's eyes when clinking glasses, seven years of bad sex will follow.

No Russian drinks vodka without *zakuski* (snacks) or a sniff of some black bread after each shot to help soak up the alcohol.

Social drinking is common in Mexico, where you can expect a boozy lunch and possibly a visit to a strip club to celebrate closing a deal.

In New York, business lunches tend to be dominated by work matters; the focus is not on the food and drink. Smoking (now banned in all restaurants and bars) is usually seen as a sign of weakness, not sophistication. The liquid lunch is a rarity: most New Yorkers stick to sparkling mineral water.

Personal face and space

Never underestimate the importance of "saving face" in Asia and East Asia. Causing embarrassment and loss of "face" can scupper the best-laid business plans.

Tactile displays of emotion (back slaps, hugs) and kissing on both cheeks are quite acceptable among men in Saudi Arabia and the Gulf.

Strict Muslim men will not shake hands with women they are not related to. As an alternative, press your palm lightly over your heart.

Personal space is not highly regarded in China: expect people to get quite close to you.

Conversely, public displays of affection or prolonged body contact would be inappropriate in Japan and Korea.

" **personal space** is not highly regarded in China "

Sartorial tips

Italians have a tendency to notice shoes straight away – keep yours shiny and in good shape.

Women travellers should dress conservatively in the Middle East (long sleeves and skirts below the knees).

In Latin American cities, high heels, short skirts and plunging necklines are quite acceptable for women.

Shoes are not worn inside Japanese houses or temples. There will be an assortment of slippers for guests to choose from. Leave your shoes (toes pointing towards the exit) at the designated spot and enter the main room. When entering a *tatami* room, remove your slippers (on *tatami* it's socks or bare feet only).

Sports

Many Germans consider chat about sport the preserve of the uneducated.

But in sports-mad Australia, it helps to know who recently won the big boat racing, rugby league football and cricket matches.

Yes and no

In Bulgaria and parts of Greece and Turkey, nodding and shaking the head have the opposite meanings they do in the rest of the world.

The Japanese avoid saying "no". "Yes" (*hai*) generally means, "Yes, I hear what you are saying".

Indians and Singaporeans also dislike saying "no". Body language will often provide more clues than what is actually said. Phrase your questions to avoid a yes/no reply.

❝ Some regard private enterprise as if it were a predatory tiger to be shot. Others look upon it as a cow that they can milk. Only a handful see it for what it really is – the strong horse that pulls the whole cart **❞**

Winston Churchill,
British statesman

❝ The chief business of the American people is business **❞**

Calvin Coolidge,
former American president